Healthcare Delivery
in the U.S.A.

Healthcare Delivery in the U.S.A.

An Introduction

Third Edition

Margaret F. Schulte, DBA

Routledge
Taylor & Francis Group

NEW YORK AND LONDON
ROUTLEDGE/ A PRODUCTIVITY PRESS BOOK

First published 2022
by Routledge
605 Third Avenue, New York, NY 10158

and by Routledge
4 Park Square, Milton Park, Abingdon, Oxon, OX14 4RN

Routledge is an imprint of the Taylor & Francis Group, an informa business

Library of Congress Cataloging-in-Publication Data
A catalog record for this book has been requested

ISBN: 978-1-032-06590-8 (hbk)
ISBN: 978-1-032-06589-2 (pbk)
ISBN: 978-1-003-20295-0 (ebk)

DOI: 10.4324/9781003202950

Typeset in Garamond
by Apex CoVantage, LLC

Contents

Figures and Tables

Figures

Tables

Acknowledgments

There were so many people along the way who influenced my commitment to this work, and though the list would be too long to acknowledge and thank each one of them, that does not diminish their influence and inspiration. My friend and publisher, Kris Mednansky, is at the top of the list of the many to whom I owe gratitude. She has been patient with always a positive word; she has let me learn just what an adventure book writing–and now a much-needed revision–is all about. I would also like to thank my many students with whom I have had the delight of working, who inspired me and who were, for me, the focal point of decades of learning, especially Hilary Tien and Uma Thandapeni who were so helpful on this project. Family, friends, and coworkers have provided the support structure on which I leaned as this process evolved, and they were always available to give feedback. Thank you to each!

About the Author

Margaret F. Schulte, DBA, LFACHE (retired) has spent her professional life dedicated to healthcare management education working with students and other professionals. She is immediate past President & CEO of the Commission on Accreditation of Healthcare Management Education (CAHME), the official accrediting body for over 100 graduate programs in healthcare management in the U.S. and Canada.

Immediately prior to this role, she served on the adjunct faculty of the Northwestern University Masters of Science in Medical Informatics program in Chicago, IL where she taught "The American Health Care System" course and earned the Distinguished Teaching Award in the School of Continuing Studies. She also served as Editor of the renowned *Frontiers in Health Services Management*, a publication of the American College of Healthcare Executives and, concurrently, as Associate Professor in the Graduate Program in Healthcare Management at Grand Valley State University in Grand Rapids, MI.

Earlier, Dr. Schulte was Vice President of Education for the Healthcare Information and Management Systems Society (HIMSS) where she was responsible for the professional education programs of this membership association of IT professionals. In this role, she led the development of annual conference education for almost 40,000 attendees, and was responsible for global healthcare IT conferences in Europe and Asia and for other educational offerings in online and seminar formats.

Dr. Schulte also held positions as vice president, research and development for the publishing division of the American Hospital Association while also serving as adjunct faculty in the Lake Forest Graduate School of Management's MBA program where she taught a course in "Health Policy, Legal, and Ethical Analysis". She began her work with professional associations as Director of Education for the Healthcare Financial Management

Association, and, earlier, her work in higher education by serving on the full time faculty of Mercer University's Masters in Healthcare Administration and Policy in Atlanta, GA.

Dr. Schulte holds a Doctorate in Business Administration from Nova Southeastern University, Ft. Lauderdale, FL and a Masters in Business Administration from Xavier University, Cincinnati, OH. In addition to authoring this book, she is a contributor to multiple books and author of publications in healthcare management.

Introduction

This book started some years ago, in work with students and so many others who have aspired to work in healthcare but have found it to be a world that is complex and mystifying. As professionals have sought careers in healthcare, whether with healthcare providers, payers, or vendors of technology, products, and services, they too often "hit a wall" of isolation and confusion in which the lingo, structures, roles, relationships, and nuances of healthcare providers can be learned only through time spent "in the trenches" gaining experience. There are also the professionals who work in healthcare, whether clinical or administrative, payer or medical manufacturing, consulting or education, government or research and want to stretch across the boundaries of their roles to new positions and opportunities. These persons also often face the complexities of what to them is, effectively, a new field of professional endeavor.

This book is for these individuals–it is meant to help them "jump start" their careers. Its mission is to provide the essentials for understanding and navigating the healthcare provider field. It is meant to provide the tools of understanding and knowledge. In it, the reader will walk through the history of the development of U.S. healthcare delivery and come to understand the highlights of a path that has shaped the strengths and weaknesses of a "system" that today is seen as too financially burdensome for the U.S. economy and in which too many do not have adequate access to care. The many venues of care delivery are described, and they provide a framework for understanding the fragmentation and complexities of the system.

Key to a successful and sustainable start in healthcare is an understanding of the wide array of people the professional will meet and work with in the provider organization. Clinicians and administrators come into healthcare from many different clinical, technical, management, and staff backgrounds. In this book, we focus on the "major players" in the clinical setting (e.g., physicians, nurses, pharmacists, and technologists), and the roles of clinicians and management becomes clear as the reader pages through the discussion of the structure of the system and its workforce.

The U.S. has the most expensive healthcare system in the world; it is also the most sophisticated in so many ways. There are many reasons behind the high cost, but the less-often measured price is in how far the U.S. has fallen behind in health status measures compared to other developed and some underdeveloped countries.

The major provisions of the PPACA have been reviewed. A major transformation of healthcare delivery has been set in motion, and focus is shifting to primary and preventive care, to population health, and to a longer view that addresses the overwhelming level of chronic conditions in the U.S. and the drain that they are on funding and on the productivity and health status of the U.S. population.

Despite its challenges, the U.S. has a wealth of sophisticated science. This book offers a glimpse into the research and medical science that are the pride of U.S. healthcare. We continue to be a world leader in finding new cures and new technologies and in understanding physical diseases and conditions. There is promise in discovery and innovation. The opportunity that medicine presents to heal and cure the diseases we know of and those we have not yet discovered is awesome.

The individual's entry into healthcare or their career shift within it will hopefully be made smoother with this book. It is meant to be a "quick read," one that paints a brief picture of healthcare in the United States today and provides a basis for interaction with providers from varied perspectives.

Chapter 1

History: U.S.A. Healthcare Delivery System

1.1 Introduction

In order to understand the fundamentals of how healthcare delivery works in the United States today, it's valuable to take a brief look backward and review the history that has shaped healthcare delivery. Today's healthcare system is the outcome of the varied ideologies and philosophies, the evolving needs and wants, and the scientific and technological advances made in current and past generations. We live with the decisions our predecessors have made, and if we are to understand the healthcare system today, then it is important to be aware of what shaped our current healthcare system for better or for worse. Every part of it has evolved from the forces that shaped it in the past. For example, some question why employers in the United States today are so embedded in the financing of healthcare through employee health insurance. In other words, how did we get to the point at which employer-based health insurance has become such a burden on employers, for some of whom its costs exceed the profit they earn? The answer is important to an understanding of healthcare financing today. The short answer to the question is: during the boom in manufacturing to meet the needs of World War II and its immediate aftermath, federal mandates restricted employers from raising wages in light of looming rampant inflation. So, employers developed a new employment strategy to attract a much-needed workforce. Private health insurance had recently evolved and employers began offering health insurance as a benefit of employment. It was a competitive move that, ironically, 75 years

DOI: 10.4324/9781003202950-1

later, has become an anti-competitive factor for those employers as they compete in international markets.

Historically, healthcare delivery traces its roots back to the fourth century B.C., to Hippocrates, who is often referred to as the "father of medicine." However, this book will not go back through the length of that rich past. We will instead fast forward to a more recent time frame and start nearer the historic time in which our country was founded.

1.2 1700 to 1850: The Early Days

In the early days of our country, there were no hospitals. People were reliant on itinerant physicians whose medical education was acquired through serving as apprentices to physicians. In most of the country, there were no hospitals. Doctors set up practices in their homes or small offices, and frequently made house calls to take care of their patients. When patients or their families could not afford to pay the doctor, bartering took place.

It was not until the mid-eighteenth century that the first U.S. hospitals were developed. Those first hospitals, unlike the hospital as we know it today, were developed to house the "insane" and the poor. Some medical hospitals began to emerge later in a small wing of these institutions. In New York, Bellevue Hospital was among the first. It was established as a public hospital in 1736 with six beds placed in a section of the New York City Almshouse. In Philadelphia, on the other hand, Benjamin Franklin helped lead, along with his friend Dr. Thomas Bond whose idea it was, the founding of the private, non-profit Pennsylvania Hospital in order to care for the poor. (1) It was built in 1752, not as an almshouse, but as a place to deliver medical care. It offered some housing to the mentally ill with beds in the basement; where persons who were deemed insane could be removed from public life.

Hospitals made it possible for healthcare workers to work more efficiently and serve more people in rapidly growing cities because their patients could be gathered in one place rather than spread throughout the city in homes and tenements. Hospitals were designed primarily for the sick poor. Examples, in addition to Pennsylvania Hospital include institutions such as the New York Hospital which was built in New York City in 1771, and the Massachusetts Hospital built in Boston in 1791. (2) Wealthy individuals still insisted on seeing their doctors and receiving care in their homes in order to avoid exposure to infections and to retain their separation from the poor.

Medical and scientific discoveries and inventions accelerated the advancement of the medical profession. In two examples: Rene Laennec, a French doctor, invented the stethoscope in 1816, particularly for use in diagnosing chest infections, and James Blundell, a British obstetrician, performed the first blood transfusion in 1818. (3) Anesthesia was discovered in 1842 when Dr. Crawford Long first used ether as an anesthetic. He had noticed in his practice that individuals injured at social gatherings known as "ether frolics" seemed to suffer no pain. Following his observation, in 1842 he administered ether to a patient and painlessly removed a tumor from his neck. (4) With anesthesia, patients were more willing to have a surgical procedure which meant that physicians could perform those procedures more readily and earlier in the case of disease or injury.

A third major development in the delivery of medical care in the middle of the nineteenth century was the initiative of physicians to organize for the advancement of medicine and medical education. In 1847, the American Medical Association (AMA) was founded. With the establishment of the AMA, a primary focus was brought to improve the medical education and training of doctors. (5) An important implication of these early days of "professionalizing" medicine was the recognition of the need for structured and scientifically based medical education, for the sharing of medical knowledge, and for the documentation of the efficacy of new procedures.

1.3 1850 to the Late Nineteenth Century: Shift from Care to Cure

During the Civil War further significant advances provided the medical profession with the opportunity to reform care delivery. The emphasis of the medical community changed with the influx of the massive numbers of sick and injured soldiers and civilians who needed urgent surgical and other medical interventions. Anesthesia had just been discovered, and chloroform and ether came into widespread use in surgical suites.

The predominant health problems of the time related to infectious diseases. Deaths from infection were about twice as common as the predominant diseases of today (cardiovascular disease and cancer). In addition to anesthesia, the discovery in 1860 of bacteria as the source of infections and understanding the germ theory of disease helped to save the lives of many injured soldiers. This discovery laid the essential foundation for later advances in the control of infection. Advancements in the understanding of bacteria progressed quickly, and the first bacteriological and chemical laboratory was organized in 1889.

The Civil War provided, as wars always have, a "research laboratory" in which medical discoveries were made. Significant advances in the operational structures of care delivery were made during the war to achieve quality and efficiency improvements, all of which have evolved further over the 150+ years since the civil war, and are still central to care delivery as we know it today. Some of the contributions of the Civil War era to medical delivery include

- development of the medical record in which data were systematically gathered
- development of a system to manage mass casualties
- design of pavilion-style general hospitals, which were well ventilated and clean
- recognition of the importance of immediate, definitive treatment of wounds and fractures
- understanding of the importance of sanitation and hygiene in preventing infection and disease
- introduction of female nurses to hospital care
- upgrading the training of thousands of physicians and their introduction to new ideas and standards of care, such as prevention and treatment of infectious disease, anesthetic agents, and surgical standards.

(6)

Following the work of Florence Nightingale (1820–1910) and other nursing pioneers, nurses were finally recognized and admitted to work in hospitals. However, their education was not yet organized within a formal educational curriculum. So, along with the recognition of nursing as a profession, a general call for improvements in nursing education was made, and the first school of nursing opened in 1872 at the New England Hospital for Women and Children. This hospital had been founded in 1862 by women to be used exclusively for women and children with a women-only staff of physicians and nurses. (7) The establishment of additional schools of nursing throughout the country followed shortly after.

Scientific advancement in medicine continued during the latter half of the nineteenth century with the discovery of radiology by Wilhelm Roentgen in 1895. Initially called roentgenology, the field advanced rapidly and with the discovery of radioactivity a year later was re-named radiology.

By the latter part of the nineteenth century, the role of hospitals began to change again. With an understanding of bacteria and its role in illness, the discovery of anesthesia and other scientific advancements, and the importance of cleanliness in the control of infections, hospitals were able to advance quality improvement in their surgical procedures. They no longer needed to simply serve as "warehouses" for the sick, and they were thus able to reshape their mission and role in society. They transitioned from a focus on maintenance care for the sick to cure and healing of the sick and injured.

In addition to scientific discoveries and to the development and transition of hospitals, a third major development would advance medical care in the U.S. during the last half of the twentieth century. This related to the training of physicians. Physician training was woefully disorganized during the nineteenth century. Aspiring physicians were primarily educated by serving as apprentices. Those who could financially afford to do so went to major cities in Europe (e.g., Paris and London) to study and advance their medical education.

The only credible medical schools that existed in the U.S. were those at The University of Pennsylvania, King's College (now Columbia College), and Harvard University, all founded in the latter half of the nineteenth century. As the country expanded and doctors were needed throughout the country, new medical schools were opened and proliferated. By 1876, 73 new medical schools were opened. They were privately owned, unsupervised, and lacked the structure needed for adequate medical training. There were no entrance requirements, and learning was completely didactic with all-day lectures supplemented with textbooks. The students had no opportunity to work with patients and there were no exams. Graduation was based effectively on the payment of fees. The medical education provided during those years was just a stumbling first step toward organized training. The early part of the next century would see significant progress in medical education.

1.4 1900 to the Mid-twentieth Century: Era of Standardization

At the start of the twentieth century and with the introduction of the "scientific method" in research, the pace of medical advances accelerated. In 1907, Ross Harrison, an American Zoologist and professor at Yale, discovered how to grow living cells outside the body. He found that nerve fibers grew from cultivated tadpole tissue, and his observations served as the foundation of today's study of nerve physiology and neurology. His achievement opened the door to the study of living organisms at the cellular level. (8) In 1919, cholesterol was found to influence coronary artery disease in humans, one of the major drivers of mortality in the twentieth and twenty-first centuries.

Sir Edward Banting led the team that discovered insulin in 1922, a discovery that had immediate impact globally for the masses of people who were diagnosed with diabetes. (9) Alexander Fleming, probably the best-known medical scientist of the era, discovered penicillin in 1928, a discovery that was to save thousands of lives during World War II after Pfizer perfected it for mass production.

Beyond medical discoveries, a small circle of medical leaders of the early twentieth century focused on the need for quality improvement in medical delivery, and, in order to accomplish this, they identified medical education as their first order of business. With the financial support of the Carnegie Foundation who had determined that improvement in medical education would be its philanthropic focus, they hired an educator, Abraham Flexner, who was known for his critical assessment of higher education in colleges in the U.S. and who had spent time studying medical education in Europe. He was commissioned by the Carnegie Foundation to perform an in-depth evaluation of medical schools in the country.

In 1910, the Flexner Report was released after four years of study under Flexner's leadership and after he visited all the medical schools in the country. He reported that (1) the quality of teaching in medical schools was poor, (2) there was an absence of hospital-based training in the medical schools, and (3) most medical graduates lacked adequate medical skills at graduation. The Flexner Report called on American medical schools to adopt higher admission standards, stronger graduation standards, the grounding of medical training in the basic sciences, and for medical students to receive hospital-based training along with their didactic classroom study. Many American medical schools fell short of the standards advocated in the report, and subsequent to its publication, and at its recommendation, most medical schools in the United States were closed. The report also concluded that there were too many medical schools in the United States and that too many doctors were being trained which also spurred the closing of medical schools. (10)

The movement towards standardization impacted not only medical training but also the organization and operation of hospitals. Minimum standards of care in hospitals were published by the American College of Surgeons at approximately the same time as the Flexner Report was being completed. Shortly after the adoption of these minimum standards, a study to examine hospitals against the standards was undertaken, and it found that of 692 hospitals examined, only 89 met all the standards. (10) This ultimately led to the establishment of what is today The Joint Commission, the first healthcare accrediting organization.

Standardization to improve outcomes of care impacted not only hospitals and physicians but also other clinical professionals. Professional licensing bodies were organized during this time, and, ultimately all professionals in clinical practice, physicians and others, were required to achieve professional licensure. The administration of licensure laws became the domain of individual states where they continue to be the domain of statewide professional Medical Boards.

Mirroring the work of the AMA, the American Hospital Association (AHA) was founded in 1898 as an organizational membership group committed to "the promotion of economy and efficiency in hospital management." (11) The AHA's efforts focused primarily on public policy on behalf of hospitals and healthcare networks and on serving as a gathering place for its executive members to share ideas and experiences.

Financially, healthcare delivery also changed dramatically during the early twentieth century. The concept of health insurance was introduced with the founding of the prototype Blue Cross plan at Baylor University in Dallas, Texas, in 1929. This plan was devised by Baylor to provide health insurance to teachers. With its introduction and success, the path was created for the rapid growth of health insurance and for the sponsoring of health insurance as a benefit of employment. With the launch of employer provided health insurance, enrollment in plans increased from approximately seven million in 1940 to 26 million covered lives by 1942. (12) With that growth, commercial for-profit insurance plans had become firmly established organizationally and as a benefit of employment.

While financing of medical care was spurred with new risk-sharing insurance plans and with the increased social acceptance of hospitals as places of cure and healing in the early twentieth century, advances in medical technology continued to impact the shape of medical delivery. More sophisticated diagnostic and surgical procedures drove increased demand for facilities and technology, and by the time of the post WWII period, the country needed to find a way to finance the construction of hospitals. The Hill–Burton Act, officially called the Hospital Survey and Construction Act, was passed in 1946 to fund the building of hospitals. Under the Act, federal funds matched by local funding were available to communities throughout the country to build and modernize hospitals. Hospitals receiving

Hill–Burton funding were required to provide care to residents of their communities regardless of their ability to pay. With a goal of having 4.5 hospital beds per 1000 population, about 6,800 hospital and long term care facilities were funded, at least in part, under the Hill Burton program by the end of the century.

1.5 Mid- to Late Twentieth Century: Advances in Science and Expansion of Insurance

Following the era of rapid growth in scientific advancement and improvements in the diagnosis and treatment of disease and injury, the standardization of medical education, the expansion of hospital facilities, the growth of health insurance, and the increased recognition of the need for government to play a larger role in assuring medical care for the poor, the late twentieth century was poised for further major change. The healthcare sector expanded, and the demand for hospital services also grew. The post–World War II era saw economic expansion and the birth of the baby boom generation. While lifestyles improved, the United States also faced the growth of chronic diseases, especially heart disease, stroke, diabetes, and cancer. Morbidity and mortality rates from these dominant diseases increased rapidly.

The latter half of the twentieth century was also a time of significant technological advances in medicine. In 1971, the computed tomographic (CT) scan was developed, and it was followed only nine years later by the introduction of magnetic resonance imaging (MRI), which gave diagnosticians the ability to "see" inside the human body in ways that no other technology had previously provided. In the 1980s, the endoscope made it possible to perform minimally invasive surgery which meant more rapid turnaround time in surgery, reduced need for hospitalization, and less pain and recovery time for patients enabling them to return to productive lives more quickly.

With the advancements in science and technology, medical specialization surged. Medical schools and teaching hospitals expanded their programs to offer increasing opportunities for specialization training. Today there are 40 medical specialties and 87 subspecialties (see Table 1.1 for examples) in which physicians can train to become Board Certified. Likewise, clinical education and specialization for other professionals such as nurses and pharmacists grew expansively during the last half of the twentieth century.

Table 1.1   Medical Specialties in the U.S.

Allergy and Immunology
Anesthesiology
Colon and Rectal Surgery
Dermatology
Emergency Medicine
Family Medicine
Internal Medicine
Medical Genetics and Genomics
Neurological Surgery
Nuclear Medicine
Obstetrics and Gynecology
Ophthalmology
Orthopedic Surgery
Otolaryngology—Head and Neck Surgery
Pathology
Pediatrics
Physical Medicine and Rehabilitation
Plastic Surgery
Preventive Medicine
Psychiatry and Neurology
Radiology
Surgery
Thoracic Surgery
Urology

Source: American Board of Medical Specialties, Member Boards, Specialty and Subspecialty Certificates; available at www.abms.org/member-boards/specialty-subspecialty-certificates/

With the proliferation of hospitals and growth in scientific advance-ments in the middle decades of the twentieth century, the need to improve financial access to medical care for the poor and elderly became apparent. The interest and commitment of the federal government in ensuring medi-cal coverage for these populations came to fruition on July 30, 1965, when President Lyndon B. Johnson signed Titles XVIII and XIX (Medicare and Medicaid, respectively) of the Social Security Act into law. With the pas-sage of Medicare (Title XVIII), individuals aged 65 years and older became entitled to the national health insurance program that Medicare continues to provide today. With the passage of Medicaid (Title XIX), the poor who met certain means-tested criteria (i.e., limited income and assets) gained access to medical care through a health insurance program in which funding is shared by state and federal governments and administered by the individual States. In the decade after the introduction of Medicare, coverage was expanded beyond the elderly to include populations with certain disabilities and those with end-stage renal disease. Today, approximately 60 million people are covered by Medicare (13) and over 70 million are covered by Medicaid. (14) These programs were a turning point for healthcare delivery in the U.S. and were followed by other programs that funded care for specific popula-tions. For example, the State Children's Health Insurance Program (SCHIP) was designed to provide coverage for children when their families' earnings exceed the earnings ceiling for Medicaid. In 2020, about 6.7 million children were covered by SCHIP. (14)

The rapid expansion of commercial health insurance through employer-sponsored programs and the passage of Medicare and Medicaid served to drive up the costs of healthcare. The increasing costs drove a rash of legis-lative and regulatory attempts to curb the rate of increase. These attempts included the passage of cost containment acts to cut reimbursement levels, of certificate of need laws to control capital spending and expansion of ser-vices, of the prospective payment system in 1983, and expansion in the use of health maintenance organizations (HMOs) and of managed care concepts.

The last half of the twentieth century also saw rapid expansion in the growth of for-profit corporate ownership of hospitals and long-term care facilities. The United States, particularly the south, had been accustomed to the presence of privately owned hospitals. In many rural communities, the sole small hospital serving a community was historically owned by one or more doctors. With the passage of Medicare and Medicaid and their guaran-teed generous reimbursement of capital costs (i.e., coverage of depreciation and interest on borrowed funds to build and expand healthcare facilities) and operational expenses (all with few restrictions), the real estate and operational values of hospital properties were enticing to investors. As a result, the for-profit investor ownership of hospitals surged in the 1970s and 1980s.

The rise of managed care in the last half of the twentieth century provided an alternative option for the control of rising healthcare costs. The concept of managed care was developed in an attempt to reduce healthcare costs through a number of mechanisms such as economic incentives for patients and physicians to use less costly approaches to care than they might otherwise use. Additionally, managed care organizations that were associated with payers, took on the determination of medical necessity of services and prescriptions. They were empowered to deny payment for care or redirect patients to less costly alternatives.

In one of its manifestations, managed care was optimized by HMOs. The Health Maintenance Organization Act of 1973 required that employers with 25 or more employees were required to offer their employees the option to join a federally certified HMO when such an HMO asked the employer to make its plan available to their employees. While HMOs were structured with far more restrictive options in the choice of providers than private insurance plans, they typically offered all-encompassing coverage of care with minimal out-of-pocket cost to the enrollee.

In discussing the rise of managed care, the rise of the integrated delivery system (IDS) or integrated delivery network (IDN) requires mention. Under managed care programs, managed care companies negotiated with providers for the rates they would pay for medical care for the covered lives enrolled in their plans. Based on the concept that the managed care company would manage the care of the patient through case management, it was assumed that lower, negotiated costs would also be managed. In response, a key strategy of hospitals was to merge into large system-wide networks in order to command a stronger negotiating position with managed care companies.

Major hospitals adopted strategies to create IDNs or IDSs by acquiring, developing, or merging with other hospitals, nursing facilities, ambulatory care centers, rehabilitation centers, specialty hospitals, diagnostic centers, freestanding laboratories and radiology centers, and physician practices. Their objective was to offer a full continuum of care so that the patients would not have to seek a different provider for any of their needs. These IDNs not only offered greater negotiating strength with managed care companies but also offered the opportunity to capture markets on the premise that they could offer the full "continuum of services" that a patient might need. They would have more doctors and services included in their networks which reduced enrollee resistance related to a reduced choice of providers in HMOs. Patients could be referred within the healthcare system for whatever they needed– theoretically simplifying each patient's life and ensuring that the patient would stay within the system. Patients were incentivized to seek care within the healthcare system of their employer's choice, or face substantial additional costs by going to a provider outside the network.

Competition between providers and payers intensified during the 1990s, as each vied in their respective spheres in healthcare delivery for the private paying patient and for the more lucrative diagnostic and surgical procedures, such as orthopedics and cardiac care. In a public policy environment that favored competition as a way to reduce costs, hospitals expanded their tertiary services (i.e., highly specialized services), with the new technologies, such as CT scanning, MRI, and cardio-vascular surgery. They also developed new specialized services to gain deeper and geographically wider market share and penetration. The medical community developed new areas of specialization as technology advanced, and that specialization sparked even more competition as hospitals sought to gain competitive advantage in those specialties.

In this environment, marketing initiatives exploded in the 1980s. Previously, marketing was generally non-existent in professional health-care management and the word "marketing" had been almost anathema in the profession. However, it rapidly became a high priority, and though the field had few healthcare marketing professionals initially, the new study of hospital marketing management exploded. College and university health-care management programs designed and implemented marketing courses in their curricula, and hospital and healthcare systems hired those trained marketing professionals as rapidly as possible. Today, the marketing depart-ments in hospitals and healthcare systems are firmly established in executive management.

Managed care also evolved rapidly during the last decade of the twentieth century furthering the competitiveness that had taken hold. Managed care organizations grew both in the corporate structure of health insurance com-panies and as independent entities. With the ability to increase enrollment among employers, the large numbers of covered lives they represented gave them the ability to negotiate prices with hospitals and doctors and, thereby, gain deep volume discounts. Providers were willing to agree to the dis-counts on the premise that they would be the exclusive healthcare provider to large numbers of enrollees and thus gain market share.

These exclusive arrangements began to erode, however, when employ-ees complained to their employers that they could no longer access their physician, hospital, pharmacy, or other provider of choice without substantial cost because that provider was not in the managed care company's network. This was a time of full employment in which employers were particularly concerned about employee retention; they responded and extended their health insurance plans to offer broader options to their employees, and healthcare costs resumed their upward spiral.

We can't leave the topic of healthcare delivery in the late twentieth century without discussion of the HIV-AIDS epidemic which was first reported on by the U.S. Center for Disease Control and Prevention (CDC) in 1981. By the end of 1984, there had been almost 8,000 HIV-AIDS cases and over 3,600 deaths from the disease in the U.S. alone. By 1999, the World Health Organization reported that an estimated 33 million people were living with HIV and 14 million had died from AIDS since the epidemic started. (15)

Another important event of the late twentieth century was the Clinton administration's healthcare reform proposal in 1993 on which the newly elected president had campaigned heavily. The plan called for universal healthcare coverage for all Americans, and as part of this, all employers would be mandated to provide healthcare insurance to their employees. The plan was actively opposed by conservatives and by the health insurance and pharmaceutical industries, and it failed decisively in 1994.

Finally, public and private investments in medical research resulted in dramatic advances in pharmaceuticals during the decades of the late twentieth century. The Human Genome Project, was established in 1990, as an international effort to sequence the entire human genome. This was accomplished 13 years later and created the path to a significant field of new and potential breakthroughs in medicine for the dawning twenty-first century.

1.6 Early Twenty-First Century: Improved Access and a Pandemic

The first two decades of healthcare in the twenty-first century have been marked by two major events: the signing of into law by President Obama of The Patient Protection and Affordable Care Act (The Affordable Care Act or ACA) and the coronavirus pandemic.

The Affordable Care Act was signed into law on March 10, 2010. With the goal of expanding access to care through expansion of health insurance coverage, the act requires every American to have health insurance coverage and provides financial help for those who cannot afford it. The ACA had significant impact on healthcare delivery by ensuring coverage for people who previously had not been covered by insurance and who were, with coverage, more willing to seek care for themselves and their families. By 2017, approximately 12 million people were enrolled in coverage under the ACA. (16)

The coronavirus pandemic, COVID-19, which is officially named SARS-CoV-2, overshadowed medicine and society in the U.S. and worldwide throughout 2020 and 2021. First identified in Wuhan, China in early January, COVID-19 was declared a public health emergency by the World Health Organization on January 30, 2020. The virus spread initially to the U.S., Germany, Japan, Vietnam, and Taiwan and, within a few months, worldwide. In the first month of the pandemic, 9,800 cases and 200 COVID-19 deaths were recorded. Within two years, over five million people worldwide lost their lives to COVID-19. In the U.S., there were over 770,000 deaths and over 47 million recorded cases in that two-year time span. (17)

Under intense demand for a vaccine, two vaccines were developed and released in December of 2020. The pace of the development of the vaccine was due in part to previous coronavirus vaccine research that had been done. The researchers did not have to start from "scratch." With the release of the first two vaccines, the effort to vaccinate the entire population accelerated in the first quarter of 2021 in an effort to effectively eradicate the disease in the U.S. As of year-end, that effort was unsuccessful. Only 69 percent of the population had been vaccinated, while millions refused the vaccine. In the populations of the unvaccinated, the disease continued to spread and surges in the numbers of cases continued to overwhelm hospitals. Worldwide, developed countries also accelerated their vaccination programs but also faced resistance. Developing and underdeveloped countries were unable to access vaccines in the necessary quantities for their populations due to the limited supply being made available to them. As the virus continued to ravage populations, concern about a possible mutation that would be vaccine resistant pressed scientists to continue to search for and rapidly assess new strains of the virus. Their mission was primarily to find new strains and modify the vaccine in an effort to keep a vaccine-resistant strain of COVID-19 at bay.

1.7 Summary

From the time of the early founding of the United States, healthcare grew and changed as dramatically as other sectors of society. Despite setbacks along the way, the advances in science moved from an understanding of sepsis and its relationship to infection and death to an ability to perform multiple-organ transplants and to understanding the human genome. Hospital organizations changed from the poor houses of the eighteenth century to the highly advanced and technologically sophisticated organizations that they are today. Physician training went from the haphazard arena of apprenticeship to the disciplined and intensive course of education of today's medical schools; payment structures transitioned from the bartering model of the early days of the country to today's multitrillion dollar third-party payment system; the legal dimension of healthcare grew and became more complex and demanding, and government regulatory involvement intensified. We discuss each of these as we continue through the next chapters.

References

1. Penn Medicine. *History of Pennsylvania Hospital.* Available at www.uphs.upenn.edu/paharc/features/creation.html.
2. J.B. Cutter. 1922 (Aug.). Early hospital history in the United States. *California State Journal of Medicine*, 20(8): 272–274. Available at www.ncbi.nlm.nih.gov/pmc/articles/PMC1517304/.
3. C. McFadden. 2018 (May 19). 15 medical inventions and discoveries of the 1800s that have come to define modern medicine. *Interesting Engineering.* Available at https://interestingengineering.com/15-medical-inventions-and-discoveries-of-the-1800s-that-have-come-to-define-modern-medicine.
4. The Editors of Encyclopaedia Britannica. *Crawford Williamson Long: American physician.* Available at www.britannica.com/biography/Crawford-Williamson-Long.
5. AMA History. Available at www.ama-assn.org/about/ama-history/ama-history.
6. F.W. Blaisdell. 1988. Medical advances during the Civil War. *Archives of Surgery*, 123(9): 1045–1050.
7. M. Reiskind. 1995. Hospital founded by women for women. *Jamaica Plains Historical Society.* Available at www.jphs.org/victorian-era/hospital-founded-by-women-for-women.html.
8. Editors of Encyclopedia Britannica. *Ross Granville Harrison: American zoologist.* Available at www.britannica.com/biography/Ross-Granville-Harrison.
9. A. Felman. 2018 (Nov. 23). Who discovered insulin? *Medical News Today.* Available at www.medicalnewstoday.com/articles/323774#next-steps.
10. H. Beck. 2004. The Flexner report and the standardization of American medical education. *Journal of American Medical Association*, 291: 2139–2140. Flexner Report. Available at https://jamanetwork.com/journals/jama/article-abstract/198677.

11. About the AHA. Available at www.aha.org/about/history.

12. C.R. McConnell. *Becoming the center of the healthcare system.* Available at http://samples.jblearning.com/9781284143560/9781284143560_CH02_Final.pdf.

13. 2018 Medicare enrollment dashboard. Latest update. 2020 (Feb. 13). Available at www.cms.gov/files/document/2018-mdcr-enroll-ab-1.pdf.

14. Medicaid and CHIP enrollment data. Available at www.medicaid.gov/medicaid/national-medicaid-chip-program-information/medicaid-chip-enrollment-data/index.html.

15. In: History of HIV and AIDS overview. AVERT. Referenced from B. Reilly. 2009. Disaster and human history: Case studies in nature, society and catastrophe. *McFarland & Co Inc.* Available at www.avert.org/professionals/history-hiv-aids/overview.

16. CMS Newsroom–Fact sheet. 2017 (Mar. 15). *Health insurance marketplaces 2017 open enrollment period final enrollment report: November 1, 2016–January 31, 2017.* Available at www.cms.gov/newsroom/fact-sheets/health-insurance-marketplaces-2017-open-enrollment-period-final-enrollment-report-november-1-2016.

17. *The New York Times.* Coronavirus United States: Daily change. Available at www.google.com/search?client=firefox-b-1-d&q=covid+deaths+in+the+US.

Chapter 2

Health Status: The Health of the Population

2.1 Introduction

The World Health Organization, in its constitution, defines health as the "the state of complete physical, mental, and social well-being." (1) Today, that definition continues to be used as the all-encompassing definition of "health." It describes the ideal state or condition of each human being. However, achievement of that ideal state, if it can ever be fully achieved, is challenging and elusive. Strategies to achieve "health" in a population are constrained by human and resource limitations within the population and by the constraints of incomplete knowledge, and of other priorities such as security, education, infrastructure, food supplies, etc. It is also constrained when there is a lack of public will to prioritize the health of the population.

In the communal life of a population, public policy is the primary arena in which health goals are established and achieved. Because of competing priorities, health is inherently defined narrowly by the limitation of resources to allocate to health and by the balancing of social, economic, and other national priorities. Implicitly, society accepts a definition of health that is within the financial capacity and will of that society and its government to provide for the health needs of its population. By their public policy decisions governments inherently define overall health status goals more narrowly than the WHO definition of "health."

"Health" also has meaning to individuals, each of whom would want to achieve perfect physical, mental, and social well-being. However, each person

DOI: 10.4324/9781003202950-2

is influenced by economic, environmental, educational, social, and genetic factors. Those who are wealthy and well educated, for example, tend to enjoy better health and better access to medical care than persons who lack financial resources, have less education, and/or do not enjoy the social status that opens doors for them. Furthermore, what is defined as complete well-being for the individual with a genetic propensity toward a particular disease may be different from other individuals. From an individual perspective, our interest is in maintaining our health and in keeping ourselves free of injury and illness, and when we suffer injury or disease, we want to know that there is medical care available and accessible. However, disparities in access to medical care exist in society, and all do not share equally in the "promise of healthcare."

From a community perspective, health status goals are achieved through environmental, educational, healthcare delivery, social, and population-based approaches. That may include cleaning up streams, creating green spaces, ensuring healthful food supplies, providing education in healthful behaviors, etc. In our various communities, we typically find homogeneous groups of people, i.e., people with something in common such as geography, race, employment, religious belief, or some other bonding characteristic. It is group behavior that enables them to achieve communal goals. Healthcare delivery is a local service, and as such it is shaped by the resources and demands of local wants and needs. Thus, the term "health" takes on different interpretations based on our individual and communal perspectives.

2.2 Health Status and Its Measures

"Health status" is one of the key measures of the health of a society. Health status is measured from a variety of factors; however, the primary measures used are mortality (death) rates, morbidity (illness) rates, life expectancy, and infant mortality rates. As Jonas and Kovner (2) said, "there are not as yet any generally accepted direct measures of health" (p. 16), so we continue to rely on the traditional measures of mortality and morbidity. Table 2.1 provides aggregate data of mortality, life expectancy and infant mortality rates in the U.S.

2.2.1 Mortality

Mortality rates are used as the measure of deaths within a population. These measures are reported by the CDC as aggregate mortality rates for the overall population and for sub-groups within the population such as those

Table 2.1   Overall Mortality and Life Expectancy in the United States, 2018

Deaths	2,839,205
Death rate	86.7 deaths per 100,000
Life expectancy (at birth)	78.7 years
Infant Mortality Rate	5.66 deaths per 1,000 live births

Source: National Center for Health Statistics. National Vital Statistics System. Mortality Statistics. Mortality in the United States, 2018. Available at https://ww.cdc.gov/nchs/nvss/deaths.htm

based on gender, race, age, and other demographic characteristics. They are also provided in more granular detail for causes of death such as cancer, coronary disease, and so on. The CDC's National Center for Health Statistics (NCHS) reports mortality rates by cause per 100,000 population. The causes of death are reported in terms of deaths as a percentage of total deaths as well as the number of deaths from each cause in the United States.

As would be expected, mortality rates have changed over the years as medical care has improved, as access to care has expanded since the implementation of Medicare and Medicaid and the Affordable Care Act, and as environmental factors have changed (e.g., reduction in environmental hazards such as poor water quality) and education and income levels have changed. On average, the U.S. population is living longer, and has fewer deaths from infectious diseases since the medical discoveries made in the early twentieth century. According to the National Center for Health Statistics, the overall mortality rate in the United States has trended downward overtime. In 1980, our overall mortality rate was 1039.1 per 100,000 population, and by 2018, the U.S. mortality rate had fallen to 723.6 per 100,000 as shown in Table 2.2. The average mortality rates of males and females have consistently differed with fewer female deaths per 100,000 on average each year than male deaths.

Mortality statistics include data that identify the causes of death in a population. Table 2.3 lists the eight major causes of death in the U.S. in 2018. These eight accounted for approximately 70 percent of all deaths in that year according to the NCHS. The dominant causes of death are diseases of the heart (cardiovascular disease) and cancer (malignant neoplasms). These two alone accounted for over 40 percent of all deaths in the U.S. in 2018. Of note, the next three highest causes of deaths each account for just over 5 percent of all deaths. These include accidents (including unintentional injuries), chronic lower respiratory diseases and cerebrovascular diseases.

Table 2.2   Mortality Rates for U.S. Population by Sex, 2018

per 100,000 population			
Year	Overall	Male	Female
1980	1039.1	1348.1	817.9
1990	938.7	1202.8	750.9
2000	869.0	1053.8	731.4
2018	723.6	855.5	611.3

Source: S.L. Murphy et al. 2021 (January 12). National Centers for Vital Statistics Reports: Deaths: Final Data for 2018. Vol. 69 (No. 13). Available at www.cdc.gov/nchs/data/nvsr/nvsr69/nvsr69-13-508.pdf

Table 2.3   Leading Causes of Death in the United States, 2018

Cause of death	Number	Percent of total deaths
All causes	2,839,205	100.0
Cardiovascular disease (Diseases of the heart)	655,381	23.1
Malignant Neoplasms (Cancer)	599,274	21.1
Accidents (Unintentional injuries)	167,127	5.9
Chronic lower respiratory diseases	159,486	5.6
Cerebrovascular diseases	147,810	5.2
Alzheimer disease	122,810	4.3
Diabetes mellitus	84,946	3.0
Influenza and pneumonia	59,120	2.1

Source: S.L. Murphy et al. 2021 (January 12). Deaths: Final Data for 2018. National Center for Health Statistics, Division of Vital Statistics. National Vital Statistics Reports Vol. 69 (No. 13). Available at www.cdc.gov/nchs/data/nvsr/nvsr69/nvsr69-13-508.pdf

In 2020 the statistics for the major causes of death shifted due to the coronavirus pandemic. In 2020, COVID-19 was recorded as the third leading cause of death in the U.S. behind heart disease and cancer. Data from death certificates filed in the U.S. indicated that COVID-19 was the primary cause of death for 345,323 people in the U.S. in that year. The total number of deaths increased from 2,854,838 in 2019 to 3,358,814 in 2020. This is a significant difference from average increase in the number of deaths in prior years.

2.2.2 Life Expectancy

Life expectancy rates are directly related to mortality. Life expectancy statistics reflect the average life span of individuals in a population from selected starting points, such as birth or age 65. In other words, if one lives to age 65, then the average life expectancy data will tell that person what life span he or she might expect from that point forward. This is an average only, and each individual life span will vary depending on factors such as health status at birth, genetics, and subsequent injury or disease as well as the environmental and other factors that impact health status. These data are used primarily to assess the overall health of a community and help to determine public policy options relative to improving health status. They are also used by insurance companies as a factor to determine premium rates for life insurance policies.

As population mortality data reflect lower average death rates for U.S. populations over time, life expectancy statistics have shown significant improvement over the past decades. In other words, people in the United States are, on average, living longer today than they did a few decades or more ago.

Life expectancy has increased dramatically since the start of the twentieth century. Thanks to advances in medicine and improvements in education and environment, people are generally living longer. The CDC reports that life expectancy at birth in 1900 was 47.3 years, but by 2018, this statistical average had increased substantially to 78.7 years. Table 2.4 provides overall life expectancy rates as reported in 1900, 2018 and selected intervening

Table 2.4   Life Expectancy at Birth for the U.S. Population by Sex, 1900 to 2018

Year	Overall	Male	Female
1900*	47.3	46.3	48.3
1950*	68.2	65.6	71.1
2000*	77.0	74.3	79.7
2018**	78.7	76.2	81.2

Source: E. Arias et al. 2021 (March 11). National Vital Statistics Reports: U.S. State Life Tables, 2018. Vol. 70 (No. 1) Available at www.cdc.gov/nchs/data/nvsr/nvsr70/nvsr70-1-508.pdf

years at birth and by sex. The 2018 data indicate a five-year-longer life span, on average, for women than for men.

Life expectancy in the U.S. is uneven not only by sex, but also for populations according to race. For all persons, the mortality rate as reported in 2018 was 78.7 years. However, for populations that are defined as "white but not Hispanic," the mortality rate was slightly lower at 78.6 years. For the black, non-Hispanic population life expectancy was about four years lower than that for all persons at 74.7 years and for the Hispanic population it was higher at 81.8 years. (See Table 2.5)

2.2.3 Infant Mortality

The infant mortality rate is another important measure of the health of a population. It is defined as "the death of an infant before his or her first birthday. The infant mortality rate is the number of infant deaths for every 1,000 live births." (3) The United States has a higher average infant mortality rate than might be expected. Jonas and Kovner describe this as an equity issue when they explain that, there is a major discrepancy in infant mortality rates among population groups in the United States based on ethnicity, education, and wealth. (2) The National Center for Health Statistics reported that the overall infant mortality rate for the United States was 5.6 per 1000 live births in 2019. When these data are analyzed relative to infant mortality among population groups by race in the United States, the statistics reveal "significant racial disparities." (4) In 2018, there were almost 21,000 infant deaths in the U.S. Of these, 10.8 infant deaths occurred per 1,000 live births among the non-Hispanic black population as compared with 4.6 among the non-Hispanic white population, 4.9 among the Hispanic population and 3.6 among the Asian (see Figure 2.1). The primary causes of infant deaths in the U.S. are birth defects, preterm birth, injuries (e.g., suffocation), sudden infant death syndrome and maternal pregnancy complications. (3) Many of these deaths could be avoided with improved prenatal

Table 2.5   Life Expectancy at Birth for the U.S. Population by Race, 2018

Per 100,000 population				
2018	*All Persons*	*White, not Hispanic*	*Black, not Hispanic*	*Hispanic*
	78.7	78.6	74.7	81.8

Source: Health, United States, 2019. Available at www.cdc.gov/nchs/data/hus/2019/004-508.pdf

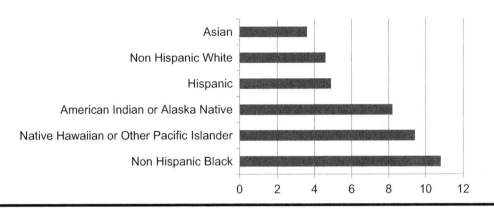

Figure 2.1   Infant Mortality Rates by Race and Ethnicity, 2018

Source: CDC. Reproductive Health. Maternal and infant health. Last reviewed: September 10, 2020. Available at https://www.cdc.gov/reproductivehealth/ maternalinfanthealth/infantmortality.htm

care and public health intervention (e.g., healthful food access in under-served areas).

With its high infant mortality rate, the United States takes a "back seat" to many other developed countries in the world. In 2020 estimates from the CIA World *Factbook*, the United States ranked 33 among the 36 countries of the Organization for Economic Co-operation and Development (OECD) in infant mortality rates (see Table 2.6).

A note on international comparisons: There may be differences in report-ing in countries around the globe and so, in some instances, the data may not be comparable. For example, in some countries, births may occur out-side the medical care system and not be reported. Additionally, the WHO requires that all children who show signs of life should be recorded. In some countries, this standard may not be followed.

2.2.4 Morbidity

Morbidity is defined as "any departure, subjective or objective, from a state of physiological or psychological well-being. In practice, morbidity encom-passes disease, injury, and disability." (5) In short, it refers to the state of health of a population. Morbidity measures the number of individuals that become ill due to a specific disease within a given population during a spe-cific time frame. Morbidity statistics identify the major illnesses affecting a population. Morbidity statistics are reported both in terms of (1) "prevalence of a disease" which is defined as the total number of cases of a disease in a population at any one time and in terms of the (2) "incidence of a disease"

Table 2.6   Country Comparisons: Infant Mortality Rate, Estimates 2020

Slovenia	1.53
Iceland	1.66
Japan	1.92
Finland	2.15
Norway	2.34
Czechia	2.42
Sweden	2.45
Portugal	2.53
South Korea	2.91
Australia	3.05
Denmark	3.09
Spain	3.14
Italy	3.14
France	3.19
Germany	3.24
Belgium	3.24
Austria	3.29
Luxembourg	3.3
Netherlands	3.45
New Zealand	3.5
Estonia	3.47
Ireland	3.52
Greece	3.61
Israel	3.62
Switzerland	3.64
Lithuania	3.66
Poland	4.22
United Kingdom	4.27

Canada	4.44
Hungary	4.69
Latvia	4.93
Slovak Republic	4.9
United States	5.22
Chile	6.68
Mexico	11.64
Colombia	12.88
Turkey	19.87

Source: CIA: The World Factbook, https:www.cia.gov/the-world-factbook/references/

which is defined as the number of new cases of a disease in a specific time frame. (5) Current morbidity data for the U.S. reflects the increasing level of chronic disease that characterizes the population. Major causes of morbidity include hypertension, injury, diabetes, intestinal infectious diseases, influenza, pneumonia, heart disease, obesity, asthma, and disability.

There is some difficulty in getting comprehensive morbidity data because accurate and complete reporting may not be available across the range of possible medical problems in a given population. For example, inconsistent reporting may occur because some patients do not seek medical care or because they are reticent to report diseases for fear of reprisal, such as loss of a job. Additionally, the data in national reports originates primarily with doctors (MDs and DOs) and insurance companies. Morbidity data are not reported from certain types of practitioners such as those performing alternative therapies (e.g., homeopathy).

2.3 Health Determinants

Health determinants are those factors that affect our individual health status and that of populations. Health determinants are composed of biological, environmental, medical, and social factors.

The Lalonde report of 1974 (issued by then Canadian Minister of National Health and Welfare, Marc Lalonde) "popularized the idea that direct medical care might be but a bit player in producing and reducing mortality." (6) In other words factors such as biology, environment, and lifestyle figure more prominently than medical care in producing health. In short, the best healthcare system available may not be the key factor in avoiding illness and injury, i.e., in reducing morbidity, in a population.

Case Example: Morbidity Increased Due to an Environmental Problem

If a group of individuals resides in an environmentally unsafe geographic area, it is likely that the health of those individuals will be at risk and that the health of a number of them will be negatively impacted by that environment. This occurred, for example, in Flint, MI when the water supply was contaminated by rusty pipes carrying water from the Flint River. This happened after the 2013 cost-saving decision of the state-appointed emergency city manager to transition the city to access water from the Flint River rather than Detroit from which it had been sourced for the prior five decades. The river water was contaminated and the pipes carrying the water were rusty. After the discovery of high blood-lead levels in children, the crisis gained national headlines, and after a citizen-led legal action and public campaign were initiated, the crisis began to be remedied.

Biological factors are those with which individuals are born. They are comprised of heredity and genetics, both of which impact the propensity to succumb to certain diseases. They also affect physical characteristics, such as height, eye and hair color, and other personal features. Advances in the science of genetics offer the potential to reshape some of those characteristics through, for example, embryonic gene transplantation.

Environmental factors are those of our physical environment, the sociocultural impact of our primary and other reference groups, economic conditions, and education that impact individuals directly. These include housing, the natural environment, the built environment (buildings, sidewalks, etc.), exposure to toxic substances (e.g., poor water quality, leaking gases, etc.), transportation, and aesthetic elements in our surroundings (e.g., lighting, trees, outdoor spaces). Studies have demonstrated that improvements in these factors support a more positive health status in any given population.

The availability of, and access to, the needed scope of medical services also influences our health status. While we in the United States are privileged to have incredibly advanced medical science available to most of our population, all of those advancements are not accessible by all of our citizens. Those who do not have access, whether due to geography or indigence, tend to have poorer overall health status than those who have appropriate access to care.

Social factors are those related to lifestyle and behavior. They include, for instance, how and what we eat, our compliance with safety laws, getting sufficient sleep, minimizing stress, performing in dangerous occupations, lack of exercise, and smoking. Among the social factors that influence health status are the socio-demographics of the population. These include:

Population growth: As the population grows, demand for goods and services increases and the need for jobs expands. If productivity or availability of goods and services does not keep pace with population growth, prices rise and incomes fall, and access to basic needs, for example healthful foods, may be diminished for some sectors of the population.

Aging baby boomers: It is expected that the aging baby boom population will require more healthcare services as their physical conditions deteriorate. While this population generally will be healthier longer into their senior years, the need for primary health services, particularly, will expand. The United States is not keeping pace with the supply of primary care practitioners needed to serve this population, and will face a significant shortage if more solutions are not implemented to incentivize medical students to focus on primary care and if funding is not made available to ensure access.

Growth in ethnic populations: As ethnic populations grow in the United States, so will the demand for services to meet their unique needs. For example, hospitals and other healthcare providers serving ethnic populations need multilingual staff and cultural understanding.

Population mobility: Population mobility, particularly as people move for jobs or to spend winter in warmer climates, impacts the need for seasonal capacity expansion in those areas. When capacity depends primarily on a trained workforce, the ability to meet those capacity requirements is challenged in areas that experience seasonal contraction and expansion of the population.

Income: The population income gap is widening between the richest and poorest Americans. Research has shown repeatedly that wealth, or lack of it, drives the extent to which a population has access to medical care. As the income gap widens, financial disparities grow. Those who have fewer resources will not be able to access care at the same level as those with abundant resources, including health insurance. This impacts not just access to medical care, but also access to nutritious food, to the best education, and to the social structures needed to support a healthy lifestyle.

Persistent poverty: As poverty and joblessness have increased, so have the ranks of the uninsured. Those without health insurance tend to put off basic screening and treatment until they find themselves in an emergency room with a serious health problem, which is far more costly than the primary care that might have prevented the advanced illness. Those without health insurance tend to seek out emergency rooms to provide basic care, knowing that the emergency room cannot legally turn them away from assessment and stabilization. This is an expensive option for providing basic healthcare service. It drives up the cost of medical care, but also results in a loss of productivity in the economy because the person who is ill tends to be less motivated or energized for optimal productive work. In both ways, it is a significant cost to society.

There is an array of factors that affect the health status of any given population. Furthermore, the presence and intensity of those factors vary by geography. While the U.S. spends an excessively high portion of its GDP on healthcare delivery, some measures of the health status of the population lag those of other developed countries, and, in some instances, of developing countries.

2.4 Summary

Health status refers to the condition of the health of a population. An understanding of health status is central to the structure of a system that can address the major health issues of a given population. Comparative health statistics paint a picture of those areas in which gains have been achieved and in which the country may need to reprioritize the public policy agenda and the use of resources. Over the past century, the life span of the U.S. population has increased significantly. However, there is still a disparity between the shorter average life span of men compared to that of women.

The high infant mortality rate positions the United States far below other countries in the world–infants younger than 1 year old have a higher probability of dying than do infants in most other OECD countries and even in some underdeveloped countries. When the U.S. population is analyzed by specific subgroups, the data indicate that persons of nonwhite ethnic populations tend to have a much higher infant mortality rate than the white population. It is these disparities toward which many public health programs are targeted and for which research has been under way to better understand and to design programs that can reverse the causes of the disparities.

References

1. World Health Organization. 2021. Preamble to the constitution of WHO as adopted by the International Health Conference, New York, 19 June–22 July 1946; signed on 22 July 1946 by the representatives of 61 States (Official Records of WHO, no. 2, p. 100) and entered into force on 7 April 1948. Available at www.who.int/about/who-we-are/frequently-asked-questions.
2. A.R. Kovner and J.R. Knickman (eds.). 2008. *Jonas & Kovner's health care delivery in the United States*. 9th ed. New York: Springer.
3. Centers for Disease Control and Prevention (CDC), Reproductive Health. *Infant mortality.* Available at www.cdc.gov/reproductivehealth/maternalinfanthealth/infantmortality.htm. Last reviewed September 10, 2020.
4. R. Kamal, J. Hudman and D. McDermott. 2019 (Oct. 18). *What do we know about infant mortality in the U.S. and comparable countries?* Peterson Center on Healthcare and KFF (Kaiser Family Foundation). Available at www.healthsystemtracker.org/chart-collection/infant-mortality-u-s-compare-countries/#item-start.
5. Centers for Disease Control and Prevention (CDC). *Principles of epidemiology in public health practice, third edition: Lesson 3: Measures of risk.* Available at www.cdc.gov/csels/dsepd/ss1978/lesson3/section2.html.
6. T.H. Tulchinsky. 2018 (Mar. 30). Marc Lalonde, the health field concept and health promotion. *Elsevier Public Health Emergency Collection*. Case studies in public health. pp. 523–541. doi: 10.1016/B978-0-12-804571-8.00028-7. PMCID: PMC7150308. Available at www.ncbi.nlm.nih.gov/pmc/articles/PMC7150308/.

Chapter 3

Components of the Healthcare Delivery System

3.1 Introduction

The healthcare delivery system is composed of an array of organizations and professionals, each of whom brings unique value to the process and the ultimate outcome of medical care. Healthcare is a local business, and as such, this sector of our society and economy is impacted by the fragmentation of many unaffiliated and unconnected care providers and payers. This fragmentation introduces a number of challenges to healthcare delivery and to the effort to achieve quality outcomes.

When we think of healthcare providers, it is primarily hospitals and doctors who come to mind. However, there are many other providers of healthcare including long-term care facilities, home healthcare and hospice services, rehabilitation programs, ambulatory care facilities, mini-clinics, mental health and substance abuse programs, and others. Over the past decades of the expansion of managed care and intense negotiation of prices by insurers, some healthcare providers have consolidated through merger, acquisition, or other strategy into integrated delivery networks (IDNs) in order to position themselves to support quality improvement initiatives, for better volume-based contracting with payers, to serve larger markets and, to support a full complement of services. In 2019, of the 5,141 community hospitals in the U.S., 3,453 hospitals were part of a larger system. (1)

In the current environment, the post–Patient Protection and Affordable Care Act (PPACA, aka health reform law), healthcare providers are integrating their organizations as accountable care organizations (ACOs) in order to serve large Medicare and Medicaid populations and further advance quality improvement efforts. In this chapter, we first discuss the types of providers and provider organizations that are available and then later discuss the integration of those providers in more detail in Chapter 4.

3.2 The Providers in Healthcare Delivery

3.2.1 Hospitals

Healthcare providers are often classified according to the types of care they provide or, considered from another perspective, by the condition of the patients they serve. Providers classified as acute care provide "medical services for persons with, or at risk for, acute or active medical conditions in a variety of ambulatory and inpatient settings." (2) In other words, acute care encompasses services that meet serious episodic medical needs, such as those arising from injuries and diseases that could be resolved through surgical, intensive pharmaceutical, and/or other therapeutic interventions.

Acute care is provided in the inpatient or ambulatory setting. Distinction between these two settings might best be described in terms of the patient: in the inpatient setting, the patient stays overnight; in the ambulatory, or outpatient, setting, the patient does not stay overnight–he or she walks (or ambulates) in and out of the medical care venue on the same day as the service is received. Hospital inpatients undergo intensive around-the-clock medical care until their discharge from the hospital.

Due to the scientific and procedural advances in medicine of the past several decades and to changes in payer policies, many procedures that once required inpatient admission to a hospital are now performed in the ambulatory setting. Robotics and endoscopy, for example, have allowed physicians to perform minimally invasive procedures often with local and/or mild general anesthetics. Further improvements in procedures have also triggered the transition of certain more invasive procedures (e.g., hip replacement) from the inpatient to the ambulatory service. After ambulatory surgery, the patient is able to recover comfortably and safely at home or, if needed, in rehabilitative services for a time.

Hospitals range in size from the very small to the major academic medical centers and government-owned facilities that may primarily serve indigents or other population groups. In all, there were 6,090 total registered hospitals in the United States in 2019, according to the American Hospital Association. These included 5,141 community hospitals, 208 federal government hospitals, 625 nonfederal psychiatric hospitals and 116 "other" hospitals. (3) Table 3.1 provides a listing of the number of hospitals by category in the U.S. in 2019.

Hospitals are typically categorized by the number of beds they are licensed to operate and, in a secondary measure, by the number of beds they have in operation, termed "staffed beds" (see Table 3.2). The distinction between licensed and staffed beds relates to the situation in which a hospital may not have all of its licensed beds in use at any point in time. When a hospital experiences an inpatient utilization level that is substantially below the licensed number of beds it is approved to operate, it will tend to take some of the beds out of service. This allows for improved operational and cost efficiency, and it allows the hospital to retain the right, under its license, to reopen some or all of the beds if and when they are needed. Table 3.2 provides the number of staffed beds by selected category in community hospitals in 2019.

Average length of stay (ALOS) is an important statistic to hospital management and to payers because reimbursement by Medicare and other

Table 3.1   Number of U.S. Hospitals, 2019

Total Number of All U.S. Hospitals	6,090
Number of U.S. Community Hospitals	5,141
Number of Nongovernment Not-for-Profit Community Hospitals	2,946
Number of Investor-owned (For Profit) Community Hospitals	1,233
Number of State and Local Government Community Hospitals	962
Number of Federal Government Hospitals	208
Number of Nonfederal Psychiatric Hospitals	625
Other Hospitals (e.g., hospital units within an institution such as a prison or school infirmary)	116

Source: American Hospital Association. Fast Facts on U.S. Hospitals, 2019. Available at www.aha.org/statistics/fast-facts-us-hospitals

Table 3.2   Number of Staffed Beds in Community Hospitals*, 2019

Total Staffed Beds in all U.S. Hospitals	919,559
Total Staffed Beds in Community Hospitals	787,995
Intensive care beds in Community Hospitals:	
Medical-Surgical Intensive Care Beds	55,663
Cardiac Intensive Care Beds	15,160
Neonatal Intensive Care Beds	22,721
Pediatric Intensive Care Beds	5,115
Burn Care Beds	1,198
Other Intensive Care Beds	7,419

Note: *Community Hospitals are defined as all nonfederal, short-term general and other special hospitals. Other special hospitals include obstetrics and gynecology; eye, ear, nose, and throat; long term acute-care, rehabilitation, orthopedic, and other individually described specialty services. Community hospitals include academic medical centers or other teaching hospitals if they are nonfederal short-term. Excluded are hospitals not accessible by the general public, such as prison hospitals or college infirmaries.

Source: AHA, Fast Facts on U.S. Hospitals, 2021. Available at www.aha.org/statistics/fast-facts-us-hospitals

payers is designed to dis-incentivize costly, unnecessary days of hospitalization. ALOS indicates how long, on average, patients are staying in a hospital as inpatients. This information is reported, not only for the overall hospital, but also more granularly for the various inpatient services within the hospital, such as intensive care units, neonatal intensive care units, orthopedics, and pediatrics.

According to the American Hospital Association's *Trendwatch Chartbook,* 2019. the overall ALOS for U.S. hospitals in 2017 was 5.4 days. The ALOS for U.S. hospitals decreased steadily from 1990, when it was 7.2 days, until 2007 by which point it had dropped to 5.5 days. Since 2007 the ALOS has remained at 5.5 to 5.4 days annually. (3) The decrease that occurred from 1990 until 2007 was due, in part, to the increased use of ambulatory and outpatient surgical procedures and to reductions in reimbursement for many inpatient stays under the prospective payment system. During the 1990s, the growth of managed care was a major driver toward reducing the length of inpatient stays in hospitals because negotiated payment plans were focused on reducing costs primarily by reducing length of stay. In the past five to seven years, prospective payment with pay-for-performance reimbursement structures have continued to place downward pressure on inpatient lengths of stay. (More on this in Chapter 8.)

3.2.2 Levels of Care

Medical care is provided at different levels of medical specialty, depending on the type, severity, and complexity (i.e., acuity) of a patient's injury or illness. These levels of care are identified by the categories of primary, secondary, tertiary, and quaternary care. While major hospitals and teaching or academic health centers may offer all four levels of care, other smaller hospitals may provide care up to the secondary or tertiary level, and in some rural areas where hospitals are small and resources are lacking, services may be limited to primary care.

3.2.2.1 Primary Care

Primary care services provide a basic level of diagnosis and treatment. In an outpatient setting uncomplicated broken bones are repaired, some basic surgical procedures may be performed, general diagnostic testing is provided, treatment of common ailments is offered, maternal and child services are provided, screening and preventive services are performed and other basic testing and procedures are offered. On the other hand, primary acute care hospitals may offer clinical and surgical services beyond those in the outpatient setting, such as appendectomies, birthing, setting of compound fractures, and other inpatient services for persons with chronic problems, the elderly, and others who may need observation and treatment in an inpatient setting. The U.S. Institute of Medicine defines primary care as "the provision of integrated, accessible healthcare services by clinicians who are accountable for addressing a large majority of personal healthcare needs, developing a sustained partnership with patients, and practicing in the context of family and community." (4)

In addition to an outpatient department (OPD), most primary care hospitals also have an emergency department (ED) in which patients can be either stabilized and admitted, sent home or, in complicated cases for which the hospital is not equipped, they can be referred to a secondary or tertiary hospital. Roemer's model of health services systems defines primary care as the entry point into the health services system, wherein:

- Illness or disease is diagnosed and initial treatment provided
- Episodic care for common, non-chronic illnesses and injuries is rendered
- Prescription drugs to treat common illnesses or injuries are provided
- Routine dental care occurs
- Potentially serious physical or mental health conditions that require prompt referral for secondary or tertiary care are diagnosed (5)

Primary care is also a designation used for physicians in specialties related to the services listed earlier. Primary care physicians include those in general internal medicine, family practice, general obstetrics and gynecology, and general pediatrics. While physicians in these specialties may also function at a secondary level of care (e.g., the pediatrician who diagnoses and treats a child with a more complicated medical problem), the dominant volume of their work is in primary care.

Primary care is offered in a variety of venues, from the acute care setting to the well-baby clinic to the home. Primary care hospitals provide basic inpatient services. Outpatient centers, ambulatory care, physician offices, community health organizations, diagnostic centers, surgery centers, home health services, and long-term care facilities are all sites in which primary care is provided. While a number of these venues of care, such as outpatient centers, provide primary care, they may also provide some secondary care services, such as invasive specialty surgical procedures. In other words, some healthcare facilities are not exclusively dedicated to primary care; they may also offer secondary care services.

3.2.2.2 Secondary Care

Secondary care includes services that are more specialized and complicated than those defined within primary care. As Barton says, "Secondary care . . . signals a higher level of intensity, often over a longer period of time, than event-specific primary care." (5) It is at the level of secondary care that most physician specialists work. These include, specialists such as ophthalmologists, gastroenterologists, orthopedists, cardiologists, urologists, and others. As with primary care, any one of these specialties is not exclusively defined within secondary care; there may be some overlap of both primary care and tertiary care in the services that they provide. For example, a cardiologist provides diagnosis at a basic level when a problematic heart condition is suspected (primary care) and also performs cardiac interventions such as inserting stents in blocked blood vessels and insertion of pacemakers (secondary care).

3.2.2.3 Tertiary Care

Tertiary care is a level at which diagnoses and interventions are yet more sophisticated and deal with more complicated surgical and other procedures. This level of care usually addresses complex conditions and intensive inpatient care. Tertiary care is typically offered in an academic medical center or large community hospital where more types of medical specialists are available and work as a team to perform surgical procedures such as transplants, open-heart surgery, neurosurgery, and specialized diagnostic procedures, such as positron emission tomography (PET).

3.2.2.4 Quaternary Care

While the term tertiary care is used to describe the highest technologic level of care available, ongoing medical advances have taken medicine beyond the realm of the historical definition of tertiary care. With the advances that medical science has made possible in the past several years, the ability to perform even more highly complex procedures in very complicated cases have also advanced. The categorization of quaternary care has been designated as a level of care in which procedures such as multiple organ transplants, specialized burn units, very complicated procedures in neurology, and other such specialized and complicated services are performed.

3.2.3 Other Categorizations of Healthcare Service Levels

Healthcare providers are further categorized based on the types and needs of the patients they are serving. These include ambulatory care centers mentioned earlier, sub-acute care, long-term care facilities, rehabilitative and other facilities and services. These subdivisions are not necessarily exclusive of one another. For example, sub-acute care may be offered in a long-term care skilled nursing facility as well as in a hospital.

3.2.3.1 Ambulatory Care

By contrast to the acute inpatient setting in which the patient is admitted and stays overnight for one or more days, in the ambulatory care setting, the patient enters and leaves on the same day. Ambulatory care is provided in surgery and diagnostic centers, walk-in clinics, and other such venues.

■ Ambulatory Surgery Centers (ASCs)

ASCs were first established in the early 1970s and experienced swift and dramatic growth in the mid to late 1980s and into the 1990s. By 2000, ambulatory surgery had become a major sub-sector in healthcare delivery. The growth in ambulatory surgery centers was due to the convergence of several factors. These include primarily:

- First, with the passage of the prospective payment system in 1983, the diagnosis-related group (DRG) payment structure was put in place to control the level of reimbursement that Medicare (and later, other payers) paid to hospitals for inpatient acute care. The DRG approach to reimbursement instituted a patient classification system that standardized payment to hospitals based on diagnosis in order to incentivize cost containment. In this regulatory environment, as noted earlier, hospitals assessed other venues in which they could provide care; they looked for ways to reduce inpatient admissions and length of stay to the extent possible. Ambulatory care was an obvious alternative and gave rise to widespread support for ambulatory surgery centers.
- Second, endoscopy and the laser had been developed, and these made minimally invasive diagnosis and surgery possible. With these technologies, many procedures that were previously performed in the hospital could be done safely in the ambulatory surgery center. Ambulatory care was not included under the prospective payment system until a decade later when the Centers for Medicare and Medicaid Services (CMS) adopted a structure of ambulatory payment groups (APGs) in order to better control costs in the burgeoning ambulatory care sector.
- Third, many specialists were eager to move their surgical practices out of hospitals where they faced "scheduling delays, limited operating room availability, slow operating room turnover, and challenges in obtaining new equipment due to hospital budgets and policies." (6) The ambulatory surgery center was their alternative for procedures that could safely be performed there.

From the mid-1980s to the late-1990s, then, was a time of significant expansion of both single-and multi-specialty ambulatory surgery centers. Despite the APG reimbursement controls implemented by CMS in 2000, ambulatory care has continued to grow. As of 2019, there were over 9,280 ambulatory surgery centers in the U.S.

■ Outpatient Departments (OPDs)

Ambulatory care is also provided in hospital OPDs. OPDs primarily provide diagnostic capabilities that may not be offered in the physician office (e.g., laboratory tests, radiology, CT scans, MRI, and other such services). They may also provide capacity for outpatient surgery and certain treatments, such as kidney dialysis, chemotherapy, and radiation therapy. Hospital outpatient departments may be offered on the campus of the hospital or in ambulatory and urgent care centers that are geographically distributed in the hospital's service area.

■ Urgent Care Centers

Urgent care centers, also known as ambulatory care centers, may be structured as:

1. Freestanding under private ownership
2. Freestanding off-campus from a hospital or health system owner
3. Situated on a hospital campus

These centers are typically open for longer hours than physician offices and are a valued community resource for afterhours primary care. They are equipped to perform radiology and laboratory procedures, and may perform minor surgical procedures that would otherwise be performed in an emergency department (ED). Urgent care centers offer convenience to the public who may otherwise have to travel a distance to get to a hospital for basic care. In addition, patients generally do not have to go through the more complicated processing and long waits that are typical of some hospital ED visits. They are a cost- and time-saving service for patients who would otherwise be seen in an emergency room and incur the related high costs.

■ Mini-Clinics

Mini-clinics are a more recent development in healthcare delivery. The first one opened in Minneapolis-St Paul in 2000. They multiplied rapidly throughout the country and within a few years were approved by employers and insurers to be included for payment in their employee health insurance plans. Mini-clinics are typically situated in pharmacies, grocery stores and other readily accessible locations across the country, most of which will also house a pharmacy. These clinics are generally staffed by a nurse practitioner, are open during convenient hours and post a list of specific services that they provide and the related fees they charge for those services. Their services meet basic needs for people with colds, flu, and other common ailments. Many also provide physicals for students who require these to participate in school athletic programs. Charges may be in the range of $90 to $130 and up, appointments are typically not required. (However, during COVID-19, many mini-clinics required appointments).

3.2.3.2 Public Health Service

While we cover public health more extensively later in this book, it is appropriate to mention here that public health clinics also provide an essential range of basic health services for persons who otherwise may lack access to care. While some public health clinics provide a full range of primary care services, others limit their services to maternal and child care, immunizations, and/or screening. These clinics are funded by federal, state, and local tax-based funds, and most utilize a sliding-fee schedule to charge the patient a portion of the established fee based on that person's income. Similar clinics are also operated by some faith-based groups in underserved areas. These are primarily financed by the faith-based organizational sponsor and through charges to Medicare and Medicaid and sliding-fee schedules related to the patient's financial resources.

3.2.3.3 Sub-acute Care

Sub-acute care provides a level of service between the acute and long-term levels of care. At the sub-acute level, patients receive care that helps facilitate their recovery from a major injury or an episode of illness (e.g., stroke). "Sub-acute care is a mix of rehabilitation and convalescent services that requires ten to 100 days of care." (7) In other words, sub-acute care is less intensive than the acute care provided in hospitals and more intensive that typical care given in skilled nursing facilities. In order to provide sub-acute care, some skilled nursing facilities have converted beds to sub-acute care in a designated separate wing with appropriate levels of staffing. In other instances, hospitals have modified or built inpatient units to accommodate the sub-acute level of care. The care provided in a sub-acute care unit includes nursing-intensive services such as intubation and ventilator support.

3.2.3.4 Long-Term Care

Long-term care technically refers to any care that requires a stay of 30 days or more. Typically, this care is provided in skilled nursing facilities and nursing homes. It is generally perceived more broadly as being "nursing home" care, which is dominantly used by the elderly and to a lesser extent by persons with disabilities that impede their performance of certain activities of daily living (e.g., dressing, self-feeding, toileting, etc.; see Table 3.3). As Sultz and Young put it: "The age, diagnosis, and ability to perform personal selfcare and the sites of care delivery vary widely for recipients of long-term care." (7) Long-term nursing care facilities may offer several levels of care, including sub-acute care, skilled nursing care, nursing home and assisted living.

Unlike acute care hospitals, most nursing facilities in the United States are owned by proprietary organizations. The CDC's NCHS reports that 69.3 percent were under for-profit ownership in 2016. Some of the remainder of nursing facilities were owned privately by church-based organizations, and still others were owned by healthcare systems or local governments. The CDC reported that, in 2015–2016, there were over 15,600 nursing homes in

Table 3.3 Activities of Daily Living

Measures	Examples of measures
Mobility	Ability to walk, get out of bed, stand from seated position
Dressing	Choosing appropriate clothing, fastening buttons
Eating	Using eating utensils
Personal Hygiene	Showering safely, nail care, brushing teeth
Toileting	Getting on and off toilet, cleaning oneself after use

Source: American Council on Aging. Activities of daily diving (ADLs), Instrumental activities of daily living (IADLs) & Medicaid. Available at www.medicaidplanningassistance.org/activities-of-daily-living/

Table 3.4   U.S. Nursing Homes Overall Statistics, 2016

Number of Nursing Homes*	15,647
Number of Nursing Home Beds	1,690,304
Number of Current Residents	1,346,941
Occupancy Rate	79.7%

Note: *The number of nursing homes excludes assisted living and similar residential care communities.

Source: National Center for Health Statistics. Nursing Home Care. Available at www.cdc. gov/nchs/fastats/nursing-home-care.htm

the United States offering over 1.7 million licensed beds with approximately 1.35 million residents (see Table 3.4). Almost half of all residents of nursing homes are 85 years or older and 72 percent are women. About 15 percent of people who are age 85 or older live in nursing homes. (8) The following sections discuss the categories of long-term care services.

Nursing Facilities

While some nursing facilities offer sub-acute care, their levels of service are defined based on the level of nursing care provided. In nursing facilities, there are two levels of service that provide clinical care by licensed nurses and a third level that provides a supportive living environment. Medicare reimburses care only in skilled nursing care. In order of clinical intensity, the three levels of service in long-term care facilities are defined as:

- *Skilled Nursing Care*: "a health-care institution that meets federal criteria for Medicaid and Medicare reimbursement for nursing care including especially the supervision of every patient by a physician, the employment full-time of at least one registered nurse, the maintenance of records concerning the care and condition of every patient, the availability of nursing care 24 hours a day, the presence of facilities for storing and dispensing drugs, the implementation of a utilization review plan, and overall financial planning including an annual operating budget and a 3-year capital expenditures program."

(9)

- *Nursing Home* refers to "a public or private residential facility providing a high level of long-term personal or nursing care for persons (such as the aged or the chronically ill) who are unable to care for themselves properly."

(9)

- *Assisted Living Facility*: "a system of housing and limited care that is designed for senior citizens who need some assistance with daily activities but do not require care in a nursing home."

(9)

Under the Medicare program, nursing facility services are distinguished and reimbursed based on the level of care the residents require as measured by their medical condition and their capacity to perform activities of daily living. Medicare pays only for skilled nursing care in Medicare-certified facilities, and that coverage starts after a qualifying stay in an acute care hospital for at least three days. This coverage is provided for services that are needed daily for up to 100 days in a benefit period. There are no annual limitations on the number of benefit periods a Medicare enrollee may have, but each <100-day period must be preceded by a three-day hospital stay. For the first one to 20 days in a benefit period, Medicare pays the full cost of coverage, and for the 21st day until the 100th day, Medicare pays all but the daily coinsurance for services that are covered. In 2019, the coinsurance required of the patient was an amount up to $170.50 per day. (10) For persons with a long-term care insurance plan, this coinsurance cost may be covered by that plan.

When individuals are admitted to the next level of care, i.e., nursing homes, they are responsible for the full cost of their care unless they are on Medicaid or have commercial insurance coverage. If they have the financial means and do not meet the poverty guidelines of Medicaid, they will "spend down" their personal wealth to cover the cost of care. Once that personal wealth is depleted to Medicaid eligibility levels, which vary by state, the patient may be enrolled in Medicaid. Medicaid pays for the cost of long-term care from that point forward so long as the patient is impoverished.

There has been controversy over this policy of impoverishment for the elderly in order for them to qualify for Medicaid coverage for long-term care. State laws are strict on the transfer of money and assets from potential or actual nursing facility residents to family or friends in order to meet the financial qualification levels to enroll in Medicaid. The principle guiding these laws is that taxpayers should not have to cover the cost of long-term care for someone who has the financial ability to pay for his or her care. In other words, taxpayers should not have to bear the financial burden of long-term care coverage through Medicaid when the individual has resources to pay for care. Many states allow the transfer of property and assets to family members if it is completed in a specified number of years prior to the time that the long-term care costs are incurred.

Nursing facility revenues come from three major sources: self-pay patients, Medicare, and Medicaid. Medicaid is by far the largest source of revenue for nursing facilities, providing approximately 57 percent of the total. Medicare pays approximately 14 percent of the total cost of nursing home care in the U.S. This is limited to skilled nursing following a hospital stay. The balance of 29 percent of nursing home costs is covered by private insurance, other payers (e.g., VA) and private individuals. (11)

Assisted Living Facilities (AFLs)

Within the classification of long-term care are also assisted living facilities. Assisted living is defined as "a system of housing and limited care that is designed for senior citizens who need some assistance with daily activities but do not require care in a nursing home." (12) AFLs offer support services in a group environment and are regulated by the state in which they are located.

With the aging of the population and the increasing longevity of the older population, along with their improving financial status and the fact that they are staying healthy longer, the demand for accommodations offering supportive care, rather than inpatient nursing care, has grown. As the older population ages and experiences a gradually diminishing physical capacity, many want to relinquish their individual homes and move into an environment in which meals and support services are provided, transportation is available, and companionship is at hand. The growth of assisted living facilities has, as a result, been dynamic since the turn of the twenty-first century. There are approximately 28,900 assisted living facilities in the U.S. They house about one million licensed beds and have, on average, 33 beds. (13)

Continuing Care Retirement Communities (CCRCs)

In some cases, developers and owners of long-term care services form continuing care retirement communities (CCRCs) which were initially designed to serve the needs of individuals at whatever their physical status might be as they age. CCRCs typically offer a full range of housing, from independent living in houses or apartments to assisted living to skilled nursing or a nursing care facility. Many also offer memory care and other specialty care units. With the availability of this range of services, a resident may move into whatever level of care he or she needs when it is needed for the remainder of their life. In other words, once individuals move into a CCRC, they are assured that, as their health deteriorates or should they need increased medical and personal support, the facility will provide the level required. The advantage of this to the resident is that he or she does not need to find a new place to live as his or her physical condition changes. Human beings tend to become increasingly sensitive to place with advancing age. The CCRC offers the opportunity to stay in place on the same campus of facilities rather than making a dramatic change of geography to find the level of care needed. Most CCRCs are fully private pay facilities and do not accept Medicaid reimbursement. There are around 2,000 CCRCs in the United States and non-profit organizations own about 80 percent of them. As they have evolved over the last three decades, they have devised contracts with their residents that offer different levels of service at a commensurate range of prices. Residents are, then, given the option to contract for a full range of services or for more limited services based on their financial status and on the range offered by the facility.

3.2.3.5 Home Healthcare

Home health agencies provide medical, rehabilitative and support care by sending caregivers into the home of the patients to provide the types and levels of care needed by the patient and ordered by a physician. Those caregivers may be registered or licensed practical nurses, aides, therapists, or others who assist the patients with their medical needs, such as monitoring blood pressure and medications and changing dressings. Patients may also receive physical, occupational, and speech therapy from licensed therapists as well as supportive services such as meal preparation, performance of light household chores, transportation, and so on.

Under Medicare, home health agencies must be certified for reimbursement, and once certified, they are designated as certified home health services. Patients who are covered by Medicare for payment of their home healthcare must meet three requirements: (1) they must be homebound, (2) a plan of treatment is prepared and reviewed periodically by a physician, and (3) the patients must require periodic or part-time skilled nursing or rehabilitation therapies. Home health agencies may be owned by hospitals, a visiting nurse association, a for-profit proprietary company, a community-based organization, or other type of entity. About 80 percent of these agencies are owned by for-profit companies. There are approximately 12,000 home health agencies in the U.S. Expenditures for home health services in 2019 were $113.5 billion. This was up 7.7 percent over 2018 expenditures. (14)

Home healthcare is predicted to grow because "the universe of Medicare beneficiaries is becoming more medically complex, with older individuals often living with four or more chronic conditions and functional limitations. At the same time, more and more hospitals and community-based referral sources are opting to send their patients to home health providers instead of skilled nursing facilities (SNFs)." (15) That expectation is driven, in part, by the experiences of the coronavirus pandemic in 2020 when virus-related mortality of persons aged 65 and older was reported in over 80 percent of all cases. Elderly residents in congregate living facilities (e.g., nursing homes and assisted living facilities) were disproportionately represented in the mortality statistics of the pandemic. As a result, it is expected that more elderly persons and their families will resist institutional care in skilled care, nursing home and assisted living arrangements to the extent possible.

3.2.3.6 Hospice Care

Hospice care is a relatively recent phenomenon in healthcare delivery. Hospice is designed to support patients and their families during the last months of the patients' life. Its growth was spurred by legislation passed in 1982 that provided Medicare coverage for patients in hospice care. This legislation required hospitals to seek out patients' wishes as expressed in advanced directives, such as DNR (do not resuscitate) options, and to encourage them to appoint someone with power of attorney to make medical decisions for them in a situation in which they cannot make decisions for themselves.

Patients admitted into hospice care are terminally ill with a life expectancy of up to six months. While in hospice care, the patient receives palliative care, which is care that addresses pain management, and other physical interventions to provide for the patient's comfort during the last months, weeks, or days of life. It is care that attempts to "relieve the symptoms of a disease rather than attempting to cure the disease." (7) The person chooses a potentially shorter life with more quality and peace away from the intensiveness of highly specialized, invasive, and expensive medical interventions that might otherwise be used. Hospice care is typically provided by a multidisciplinary team consisting of physicians, nurses, counselors, psychologists, social workers, and therapists. Typically, all medical supplies and drugs, as well as the required professional nursing and supportive services, are financially covered by Medicare and other payers, with smaller co-payments by the patient. Hospice supports both the terminally ill patient and the family.

The number of hospice programs in the U.S. grew from 3,100 in 2000 to 4,300 in 2017 when they served 1.49 million patients. Approximately 63 percent of hospices are under for-profit ownership. (15)

3.2.3.7 Respite and Day Care

Respite care and adult day care are two valued services for family caregivers. Adult day care is a service in which an elderly person, or someone whose physical condition requires continuous care, is cared for outside the home in a group setting during the workday or any other scheduled period. In a typical scenario, the person who is "dropped off" at the day care center is provided supportive assistance while the full-time caregiver goes to work. Respite care, on the other hand, is provided in order to support the caregiver for whom the demands of constant care giving can be stressful and very time-consuming. Respite care provides a setting in which the one being cared for can stay in a safe supportive place while the caregiver has time to perform errands or travel or "get away" for several days or a week. Adult day care services are typically tied to a nursing facility and, in some cases, to a community senior center. Respite care, because it is overnight care, is typically a service offered by a nursing facility.

3.2.3.8 Rehabilitation

Rehabilitation services provide physical, occupational, and speech therapies for patients who have suffered an illness or injury that leaves them with some level of physical disability. Rehabilitation is designed to provide services that help the patient achieve their optimal level of physical function following an injury of illness. While there are a number of hospital-based inpatient rehabilitation facilities (IRFs) throughout the country, rehabilitation is more generally provided on an outpatient basis and is included in the services that nursing care facilities provide to patients. In rehabilitation facilities, a physiatrist is the physician specialist who provides medical service and leadership to the rehabilitation department. The team includes physical, occupational, and speech therapists as well as social workers and counselors. Currently there are approximately 200 rehabilitation hospitals in the United States. These may be either freestanding or in a designated section of an acute care hospital.

3.2.3.9 Emergency Services

Emergency services (EMS) are part of healthcare delivery in rural and urban areas across the country, and they are also a key part of the fabric of healthcare. Their organization varies from a volunteer model to a corporate model. Their locus also varies. Emergency services are frequently housed with other community services, such as a fire department, and in yet other instances they are situated within the campus of hospitals and medical centers. Volunteer emergency services often do not have paramedics and EMTs (emergency medical technicians) on-site. Instead, volunteers stay "at the ready" and respond to 911 calls. In other instances, full-time, round-the-clock paid professionals staff the emergency service. Staffing may also vary in the level of training required. Frequently, paramedics are not available or assigned to ride to the scene of an emergency unless the dispatcher notes that the extent of illness or injury requires the more highly trained professional.

3.2.3.10 *Mental Health and Substance Abuse*

According to Johns Hopkins Medicine, "An estimated 26% of Americans ages 18 and older–about one in four adults–suffers from a diagnosable mental disorder in a given year." (16) Healthcare provider organizations that provide mental health services are typically either psychiatric facilities or substance abuse facilities. Mental healthcare may be provided on either an inpatient or an outpatient basis. The dramatic improvements in psychotropic drugs of the past several decades have provided the opportunity for mental healthcare to move primarily to an outpatient setting.

Mental health provider organizations may be owned privately and as free-standing facilities by for-profit entities, by faith-based or other non-profit organizations. Others are based in acute care hospitals, and in some cases, mental health facilities are owned by state or local governments. Many of these facilities specialize in adolescent or adult care; others specialize in substance abuse treatment. Payment for mental healthcare has been limited under both public and private plans, and frequently further limited by a focus on outpatient treatment.

3.3 Summary

This chapter has provided the descriptions and essential characteristics of the various organizational entities through which healthcare is delivered in the United States. These are the entities that play central roles in healthcare delivery. There are several other venues that support healthcare, including alternative and holistic medicine centers, chiropractic and podiatric care, vision care centers, and others. These are of significant benefit to many consumers, and many of their services are included under third-party payer arrangements. While the latter are not discussed in this book, they certainly merit acknowledgment, and it should be recognized that they are growing in both number and volume of service in the United States. Private physician practices are also an important part of the continuum of medical care and will be discussed in Chapter 5.

References

1. American Hospital Association. *Fast facts on U.S. hospitals, 2021.* Available at www.aha.org/statistics/fast-facts-us-hospitals.
2. A.R. Kovner and J.R. Knickman. 2008. *Jonas and Kovner's health care delivery in the United States.* 9th ed. New York: Springer, p. 213.
3. American Hospital Association. 2019. *Trendwatch chartbook.* Available at www.aha.org/system/files/media/file/2019/11/TrendwatchChartbook-2019-Appendices.pdf.
4. Institute of Medicine (US) Committee on the Future of Primary Care; M.S. Donaldson, K.D. Yordy, K.N. Lohr ,et al., editors. *Primary Care: America's health in a new era.* Washington, DC: National Academies Press (US); 1996. 2, Defining Primary Care. Available from: https://www.ncbi.nlm.nih.gov/books/NBK232631/
5. P.L. Barton. 2010. *Understanding the U.S. health services system.* Ann Arbor, MI: Health Administration Press, Ch. 13, p. 331 and Ch. 14 p. 339.
6. Ambulatory Surgery Center Association. *History of ASCs.* Available at www.ascassociation.org/advancingsurgicalcare/asc/historyofascs.
7. H.A. Sultz and K.M. Young. 2009. *Health care USA.* Sudbury, MA: Jones and Bartlett Publishers, pp. 86, 98, and 302.
8. National Center for Health Statistics. *Nursing home care.* Available at www.cdc.gov/nchs/fastats/nursing-home-care.htm.
9. Merriam-Webster. *"Skilled nursing facility"; "nursing home"; "assisted living."* Available at www.merriam-webster.com/medical/skilled%20nursing%20facility.
10. CNS. *Medicare coverage of skilled nursing facility care.* Available at www.medicare.gov/Pubs/pdf/10153-Medicare-Skilled-Nursing-Facility-Care.pdf.
11. American Health Care Association. 2015 (June). *Skilled nursing care centers.* Available at www.ahcancal.org/Data-and Research/Documents/FastFacts_SNCCs.pdf.
12. Merriam-Webster. *Assisted living.* Available at www.merriam-webster.com/dictionary/assisted%20living. Accessed April 14, 2021.
13. AHCANCAL. *Facts and figures.* Available at www.ahcancal.org/Assisted-Living/Facts-and-Figures/Pages/default.aspx.
14. R. Holly. 2020 (Dec. 16). National home health spending reaches all-time high of $113.5 B=billion. *Home Health Care News.* Available at https://homehealthcarenews.com/2020/12/national-home-health-spending-reaches-all-time-high-of-113-5-billion/.
15. National Hospice and Palliative Care Organization (NHPCO). 2019 (July 8). *A re-envisioned report on hospice access and usage in the U.S.* Available at www.nhpco.org/nhpco-releases-updated-edition-of-hospice-facts-and-figures-report/.
16. Johns Hopkins Medicine. *Mental health disorder statistics.* Available at www.hopkinsmedicine.org/health/wellness-and-prevention/mental-health-disorder-statistics.

Chapter 4

Structure of Healthcare Delivery

4.1 Introduction

In the last chapter, we discussed the various components or types of healthcare providers. Although they were described individually, they also comprise the continuum of care. "The continuum of care is a concept involving an integrated array of health services spanning all levels of intensity of care." (1) It requires the availability of a full range of services and the mechanisms to integrate those services. These mechanisms are primarily "inter-entity planning and management, care coordination, case-based financing, and integrated information systems." (2) In other words, all services in the continuum work together, share information, and are systemically integrated.

The continuum of care is meant to improve access and quality of care for the patient. It includes the various types of providers of care that a patient might need to access as they go through life and through incidences of illness or injury. For example, the patient who has had a stroke may initially access care through the emergency department of a hospital, from which he or she may then transfer to an intensive care unit in the hospital, then to a subacute unit, then to a rehabilitation facility, and finally perhaps home to receive care by home health providers. Each of these provider entities may be under different ownership and corporate structures, but in order for the continuum to be effective, each must be linked to the other through the four mechanisms noted earlier. For this reason, providers (mostly hospitals) have integrated the full range of services within one corporately owned organization known as a health system or integrated delivery network (IDN) or integrated delivery system (IDS).

DOI: 10.4324/9781003202950-4

When a true continuum of care is lacking, patients navigating the process of care must create a new relationship with each provider, including new paperwork, new insurance approvals, and new protocols of care. While each physician visit or service would ideally be informed by the work of the previous provider (e.g., the case of the patient with a broken bone must find a physical therapist and ensure that the therapist has adequate information from the medical record and that they accept the patient's insurance), comprehensive transitions of care protocols may not exist to make the process smooth. In this event, quality is at risk. Lacking electronic communication through a shared EHR, often means that the transition of care and of information among providers is fraught with error and miscommunication.

The development and implementation of integrated healthcare IT systems lagged most other sectors of the U.S. economy until the early twenty-first century. Their implementation was accelerated significantly with the passage of the American Recovery and Reinvestment Act (ARRA) following the 2008 recession. One of the provisions of ARRA, the Health Information Technology for Economic and Clinical Health Act (HITECH) offered incentive payments to hospitals and physicians to implement certified electronic records. By 2015, 96 percent of non-Federal acute care hospitals in the U.S. had adopted a certified EHR. (3) The Patient Protection and Affordable Care Act of 2009 (Commonly known the ACA) further addresses the continued development of the interoperable EHR through its provisions for the development of accountable care organizations (ACOs) and through its support for the implementation of integrated healthcare IT systems.

In this chapter, we discuss the linkages, and lack thereof, among the various providers of care and address the role of reimbursement policy and information technology in integrating providers in order to reduce costs and improve quality of care. First, the organizational structures under which providers function are discussed. Following that, the classifications of providers that were introduced in Chapter 3 are explained further, and the work of care coordination among providers is addressed.

4.2 Hospital Classifications

In Chapter 3, we discussed classification of healthcare providers based on the services they provide. All the provider organizations identified in Chapter 3 may also be classified in a number of other ways, including by (1) ownership, (2) tax status, and (3) geographic location. Each has its own unique impact on the operation of the hospital, and all apply to every hospital. For example, a hospital owned by a faith-based group may be tax-exempt, it may be situated in a rural area, and it may be the only general acute care hospital serving the area. We discuss each classification in turn.

4.2.1 Ownership

Terms that are often used to describe healthcare organizations are *private* and *public* when describing healthcare providers. Most hospitals and organizational providers of care are considered private hospitals. Those that are not private are hospitals operated by governmental entities such as the Veterans Affairs (VA), Indian Health Services (IHS), county and municipal hospitals (e.g., Grady Health System in Atlanta, John H. Stroger, Jr. Hospital in Chicago), and prison hospitals. Public hospitals are organized and operated under the authority of a government entity.

Hospitals and other healthcare providers are frequently characterized by the term "community" hospital. The term *community hospital* may be used for hospitals that are founded and owned to serve the local community, whether by a faith-based organizations or by a for-profit company. It is broadly applied to those hospitals that serve the locality in which they operate and is typically used in contrast to the categorization of hospitals that serve a more widespread community such as academic medical centers or teaching hospitals.

4.2.1.1 Private Healthcare Organizations

Private healthcare entities are any that are not owned by a public governmental entity. *Private* in this classification means that they are owned and operated under the auspices of a non-profit or an investor organization. Some are organized and operated under the auspices of a community. Having been founded by community leaders (such as a school might be established), the assets are owned by that community and function under the governance structure of that community. In this instance, typically, an initial board of directors is appointed to the healthcare organization by the county or community elected leaders, and that board operates continuously. Members have term limits, and when a member's term expires, they are replaced by board selection and appointment of new members from the community.

Some private hospitals are owned by *for-profit corporations*. These corporations may be owned by a group of private individuals or formed as public corporations, with their stock trading on a public stock exchange. Privately owned hospitals have been organized throughout history since the founding of hospitals in the U.S. Many of the early hospitals in the U.S. were founded and operated by the doctor(s) in the area the hospital serves. Over time some of these hospitals grew, and with the passage of Medicare and Medicaid in the 1960s, hospitals became more lucrative under the generous reimbursement schedules of these programs. Subsequent to the implementation of Medicare and Medicaid, the investor-owned hospital sector grew and expanded. Today over 2,900 hospitals in the U.S. are investor-owned.

Many private healthcare organizations are *faith-based organizations.* Historically, a number of faith-based organizations developed hospitals and clinics to care for persons in a locality for which the organization determined that a need and an opportunity existed to serve both the spiritual and physical needs of their faithful. Faith-based hospitals are operated by organizations under the auspices of the Baptist, Methodist, Lutheran, Presbyterian, Jewish, and Catholic and other faiths. They do not limit their care to persons of their religious beliefs, and they operate competitively as do for-profit health systems. About 14 percent of the hospitals in the United States are owned by faith-based organizations "which are among the largest provider organizations in the country" (see Table 4.1).

4.2.1.2 Government/Public Hospitals and Clinics

Government/public hospitals and clinics are those that are operated by federal, state, or local governments. Public hospitals are organized and operated under the authority of the respective government entity and shortfalls in their financial operations are paid with taxpayer dollars. Many local public hospitals originated as places for indigents whose care was the responsibility of the local government, and some have evolved over time to state-of-the-art tertiary healthcare organizations. While they continue to serve primarily indigent persons and those on Medicaid, many of them have developed top-rated emergency departments and trauma centers and other specialized services. They accept all patients that are admitted by a physician on their medical staff and their emergency rooms are open to all people regardless of ability to pay.

Other public hospitals and medical services are those owned by the Department of Veterans Affairs (VA), which operates them for retired members of the military for whom care is financed by the VA. A limitation for retired military individuals is that, depending on where they live, they may have limited geographical access to their VA hospital. Overall, the VA

Table 4.1   Largest Health Systems in the U.S., 2019

Name of System	Corporate Headquarters	Number of Hospitals
HCA Healthcare	Nashville, TN	185
Ascension Health	St. Louis, MO	151
CommonSpirit Health	Chicago, IL	142
Community Health Systems	Franklin, TN	105
Trinity Health	Livonia, MI	92
LifePoint Health	Brentwood, TN	86
Tenet Healthcare	Dallas, TX	65
Vibra Healthcare	Mechanicsburg, PA	65
Providence St. Joseph Health	Renton, WA	51
Atrium Health	Charlotte, NC	50
AdventHealth	Altamonte Springs, FL	50
Baylor-Scott & White Health	Dallas, TX	48
Bon Secours Mercy Health	Cincinnati, OH	48
Prime Healthcare	Ontario, CA	45
Sanford Health	Sioux Falls, SD	44
Mercy	St. Louis, MO	41
UPMC	Pittsburgh, PA	40
Kaiser Permanente	Oakland, CA	39
MercyOne	Clive, IA	39
Steward Health Care	Dallas, TX	37
Christus Health	Irving, TX	35
Avera Health	Sioux Falls, SD	33
Ardent Health Services	Nashville, TN	30
Great Plains Health Alliance	Wichita, KS	29
Texas Health Resources	Arlington, TX	29

Source: L. Dryda. 2020 (Jan. 20). 100 of the largest hospitals and health systems in America, 2019. *Beckers Hospital Review*. Available at https:www.becker-shospitalreview.com/lists/100-of-the-largest-hospitals-and-health-systems-in-america-2020.html

provides 1,283 outpatient clinics and 171 medical centers serving approximately nine million enrolled Veterans each year. (4)

Government or publicly owned providers of care are also responsible for healthcare on Indian reservations. The federal government's commitment to the American Indians and Alaska Natives is enshrined in Article 1, Section 8 of the U.S. Constitution. The Indian Health Services (IHS) is an agency within the Department of Health and Human Services that provides healthcare for 2.56 million American Indians and Alaska Natives who belong to 574 federally recognized tribes. The 12 IHS area offices administer 24 hospitals, 51 health centers, and 24 health stations. The IHS received a budget appropriation of $6.0 billion in FY2020. (5)

4.2.2 Tax Status: Taxed or Tax-Exempt

Healthcare organizations that are established as for-profit entities typically are eligible to receive tax-exempt status; other not-for-profit entities, on the other hand, function as taxable organizations. For-profit entities pay federal, state, and local taxes unless they are given a specific tax exemption by the respective level of government under which they operate (e.g., some may be exempt from paying property taxes for a period as an inducement to locate in a given municipality or county/parish).

To the nonprofit, or tax-exempt, healthcare organizations, the tax benefits are more expansive than any given to taxable entities. Tax-exempt organizations may qualify for favored tax treatment under federal as well as a variety of state and local income, property and sales-tax laws. In addition to tax exemptions, nonprofit status allows hospitals to benefit from tax-exempt bond financing and to receive charitable contributions that [may be] tax-deductible to the donors. (6)

In the case of healthcare organizations that hold property tax exemption, the community's expectation is that the organization will, in return provide "community benefit." That is, in return for the tax subsidy, the tax-exempt entity is expected to give back to the community, i.e., to provide services to the community at no, or reduced, cost. Community benefit is typically comprised of programs such as free care for indigents or care based on a sliding fee schedule that reflects the individual's ability to pay. It may also include the cost of community services such as education programs in prevention (e.g., smoking cessation), screening clinics, and other healthcare services.

There is no set standard for the financial levels at which a community benefit should be established for tax-exempt hospitals. Some states or localities expect tax-exempt hospitals to provide free services equal to 2 to 7 percent of their revenue. While there is no consensus on a standard yet, the IRS includes Schedule H of the 990 Form that nonprofits are required to complete and submit. This schedule requires hospitals to fully disclose their community benefits for tax years beginning in 2009. Bad debts and Medicare discounts are not eligible for consideration as community benefits. (7)

As local governments face revenue shortfalls and increasing demand for tax revenues to support infrastructure and public services, they will continue to examine the value they receive from their local nonprofit hospitals. They will question whether or not the community benefit provided by the non-profit hospital(s) adequately meets the value of foregone taxes. In a community's pressing financial circumstances, it is compelling for local governments to review the community service value that is provided in return for the tax exemptions they provide.

4.2.2.1 Tax-Exempt, Not-for-Profit Healthcare Providers

Not-for-profit hospitals and health systems operate under the financial principle that no net revenue or profit is paid to individuals or organizations based on investment in, or ownership of, the nonprofit organization. There is no personal financial investment ownership of the nonprofit. The nonprofit may record a net income on its income and expense statement, but all net income is retained and reinvested in the organization; it is not paid out as investment income, nor may it inure to the benefit of any individual.

Among its expenses, the nonprofit healthcare provider employs management professionals and support and clinical staff to carry out the duties and tasks required to run a complicated organization. These staff members include everyone from the president/CEO to doctors, nurses, technologists, therapists, pharmacists, dietitians, maintenance, and office personnel. Each of them is paid typically competitive salaries for their respective geographic area or region. Staffing is among the major line item expenses of a healthcare provider.

Some individuals have the perception that if a hospital or any other medical provider is established as a nonprofit, it must not make profit. To the contrary, the nonprofit establishes fees that are competitive with other providers in its area and structures its budget to achieve a profit after all expenses are paid or accounted for.

In some cases, nonprofit healthcare systems may own a for-profit entity, such as a managed care organization or a real estate holding company in which property is held for future use and/or rented out on a for-profit basis. In these cases, the subsidiary for-profit company is required to pay taxes on its net revenues or profit.

4.2.2.2 Taxed, For-Profit Healthcare Providers

For-profit hospitals have existed in the United States for decades. In the early history of the United States, many of the early U.S. hospitals were founded and owned by physicians. The origin of the for-profit multihospital corporation dates back to the 1960s when several investor-owned companies such as Hospital Corporation of America (known today as "The Hospital Company") were founded. Entrepreneurial investors found fertile ground primarily in the South where many small community hospitals were owned by physicians or by small towns. With the advent of Medicare and Medicaid and the proliferation of commercial health insurance through employer funding, and in a time when hospital bills were paid with few questions by these payer organizations, hospitals had strong equity value and provided opportunity for profitability. When the physicians or community owners faced the increasing complexity and cost of running a hospital as technology improved, medical advances progressed and payment systems changed, the sale of the hospital became an attractive alternative. On the one hand, the hospital's equity value had increased under the new Medicare and Medicaid programs and on the other hand local governments had found that the demands for funding for other community services, such as improved schools, roads and jails had grown beyond their budgets. The income from the sale of the hospital to a for-profit hospital operator provided the funds for other essential community services while maintaining the hospital in the community.

Today there are a number of for-profit hospital companies, both large and small. They own varying numbers of hospitals, but, typically, those hospitals are geographically dispersed and not networked or fully integrated for the sharing of patient and financial or other operational information. They operate under the same rules and regulations as nonprofit hospitals; however, a key purpose of their ownership is that they return a profit to investors.

4.2.3 Geography

There are two geographic classifications of hospitals: urban and rural.

Urban: Hospitals classified as urban hospitals are those that are located in a metropolitan statistical area of 50,000 or larger population.

Rural: Rural hospitals are those that are not located in a metropolitan statistical area.

Each of these classifications has implications for the way in which Medicare reimbursement is calculated. In part, that calculation looks at the different costs of urban and rural operations. Many rural hospitals are smaller primary care facilities and do not have the revenue-generating capacity of their urban counterparts, particularly in the more lucrative specialty services such as cardiology and orthopedics. They also generally do not serve more complicated and specialized patient admissions. As small hospitals, highly dependent on Medicare and Medicaid, many of these hospitals need proportionately higher reimbursement in order to remain operational.

Rural hospitals may be designated as critical access hospitals (CAHs) under Medicare. The CAH designation was established under the 1997 Balanced Budget Act. Because these facilities provide a critical source of access to care for the residents of their geographic area and based on the premise that there is no other access point to inpatient medical care in the area, these hospitals are reimbursed by Medicare on a cost-based system rather than on a prospective payment or diagnosis-related group basis. The criteria for CAH designation include requirements that the hospital may be no larger than 25 inpatient beds, have no more than an average 96-hour length of stay, and generally be located 35 miles from another hospital. As of July 2019, there are 1,350 rural hospitals that are designated as CAHs. (8)

4.3 Types of Hospitals

4.3.1 General Acute Care Hospitals

Also known as medical surgical hospitals or "short stay," these healthcare providers offer a range of inpatient services from surgery to pediatrics, obstetrics (labor and delivery), orthopedics, intensive and perhaps cardiac care intensive units, diagnostic services, and outpatient services. General acute care hospitals are defined in part by the kinds of services they perform and by the fact that their ALOS is less than 30 days. As noted in Chapter 2, their average length of stay was 5.4 days in 2017. They may be organized as voluntary nonprofit entities, as private for-profit businesses, or as public organizations owned and managed by a public governing body (federal, state, county, or local government).

4.3.2 Academic Medical Centers and Teaching Hospitals

Two other types of general acute care hospital are the academic medical center and the teaching hospital.

The organizational structure of *academic medical centers* (AMCs) blossomed in the 1960s when federal legislation and research grants supported the advancement of research and teaching in medical schools. In 1965, Public Law 89-239 authorized the funding and establishment of Regional Medical Programs (RMPs). The objective of the program was to "encourage and assist in the establishment of regional cooperative arrangements among medical schools, research institutions and hospitals for research and training, including continuing education, and for related demonstration of patient care." (9) This provided an impetus for medical schools and hospitals to organize as one legal entity–the AMC.

As hospitals and medical schools organized themselves under one governance structure, i.e., as academic medical centers, they provided the infrastructure for research and advanced medical learning. The hospital provided the "laboratory" for research and for medical students' clinical exposure to medical practice during their clinical rotations and internships, and the medical school provided the academic environment for didactic learning.

Over time, many academic medical centers have expanded into becoming broader academic health centers as they added nursing schools, schools of pharmacy, medical technology programs, and educational programs for other allied health disciplines. In various organizational arrangements, they either develop their own on-campus allied health school or align with local colleges and universities to provide classroom training while the medical center provides clinical practice sites for students.

Teaching hospitals operate in affiliation with medical schools and/or an academic medical center in order to provide hands-on clinical training for physicians and other clinicians. In this arrangement, the hospital and the medical school are separate entities in contrast to the AMC in which they are structured under one organizational entity. The U.S. healthcare system relies heavily on teaching hospitals and their clinics, emergency departments, ambulatory care centers, chronic care facilities, hospices, and individual and group practices for the clinical education of medical students and physician residents.

According to the Association of American Medical Colleges (AAMC), there are 155 accredited allopathic and 48 osteopathic medical schools in the U.S. In 2006, the AAMC called for a 30-percent increase in enrollment in medical schools based on projections of a future shortage of physicians. As a result, over the past 15 years, there has been a significant expansion of medical schools. Class sizes at medical schools were increased and 29 new allopathic and 17 osteopathic medical schools were opened in the intervening years up to the present. (10)

4.3.3 *Specialty Hospitals*

Specialty hospitals have been a part of the fabric of U.S. healthcare delivery for the past century. They are hospitals that specialize in performing a limited range of specific medical diagnoses and treatments. Early specialty hospitals were those that served individuals with mental illness and women. Today, specialty hospitals are found on the campuses of major medical centers or as free-standing entities geographically removed from the medical center. They typically focus on any one of a range of services such as pediatric care, physical rehabilitation, psychiatric services, cancer, cardiology, orthopedics, mental health, substance abuse or another service. Some specialty hospitals are not owned by, or affiliated with, a medical center or health network, but they are owned by private investors. There are a number of for-profit chains that own mental health service hospitals and outpatient treatment centers and still others offering substance abuse treatment. For example, Reflections, Vertava Health, and Caron Treatment Centers are private investor-owned companies providing specialty hospitals that offer substance abuse addiction treatment.

4.3.4 *Mental Health Hospitals*

Mental health hospitals may be owned by either a governmental or a private entity. They are also known as behavioral health facilities. Historically, it has been the role of state governments to provide needed mental healthcare services within their respective states for persons in need who are unable to pay for these services. Consequently, states across the country developed large mental health facilities during the early to middle twentieth century; many of these facilities operated a thousand or more beds and were often utilized as "warehousing" venues for persons with mental illnesses or other conditions that affected their behavior.

The federal Mental Health Centers Act of 1963 provided funding for community mental health centers and research facilities to facilitate and expand support for mental health patients in their communities. A process of "deinstitutionalization" of mental health patients and their reintegration back into society was accelerated with the development of psychotropic drugs and additional federal support through Medicaid programs. As state hospitals closed their doors, many of the resident patients of these defunct facilities were helped to find community living arrangements and were supported with additional federal funding.

Most states continue to operate mental health facilities; however, these are more scaled back in size for inpatient care, and most of them emphasize outpatient and day treatment. More recent advances in drugs to treat mental health conditions have enabled states to effectively address the needs of patients in this less institutionalized setting.

Mental health inpatient facilities are owned and operated by both nonprofit and for-profit companies. These businesses may specialize in mental health and/or substance abuse treatment and some sub-specialize in treatment of just children and/or young adults. Many of these private companies own facilities and outpatient services with facilities geographically dispersed across the country or in certain regions. Statista reports that in 2019 there were 708 psychiatric facilities in the United States of which 325 were listed as private for-profit hospitals, 169 as private nonprofit and 214 under the aegis of a public agency or state government department. (11)

4.4 Hospital Operations

There are three areas that are essential to gaining an understanding of how hospitals function: (1) the structure of the hospital-physician relationship, (2) the structure of the integrated delivery network (IDN), and (3) the structure of reimbursement for services (i.e., the business model of healthcare). The third area is discussed in Chapter 8. In this chapter we focus on the hospital–physician relationship and the structure of the IDN.

4.4.1 The Structure of the Hospital–Physician Relationship

In today's dynamic and changing healthcare environment, the relationship between doctors and hospitals is undergoing fundamental change. The old relationship of the independent physician working in the independent hospital has given way to a deeper integration and collaborative structure between the two. Reimbursement structures under bundled payments and through Accountable Care Organizations (ACOs), and other quality and cost control mechanisms, are designed to reward providers for coordinated care and for improving the health of defined population groups. In order to take advantage of ACO reimbursement structures, hospitals and doctors are required to coordinate care, share patient information, institute programs to reduce unnecessary readmissions to the hospital, improve care quality based on specific metrics, and reduce duplication of services and diagnostic testing. In short, hospitals and doctors have been pressed into new collaborative arrangements.

This has manifested itself in several trends. There are few independent small physician practices remaining. Physicians are instead opting to sell their practices to hospitals or practice management organizations (PMOs) and placing themselves on their employer's payroll. While they practice with apparent independence, they are required to meet quality metrics established by the hospital or PMO (e.g., patient satisfaction and case load metrics). The American Medical Association (AMA) reports that

> in 2018, 47.4% of practicing physicians were employed, while 45.9% owned their practices. . . . The new ownership figures are a milestone, marking the first time the number of employed physicians is greater than the number of those who own practices.
>
> (12)

Independent or physician-owned practices still operate under financial arrangements that have characterized the hospital-physician relationship historically. Physicians who own their practices admit patients to the hospital and order tests or procedures in the hospital, but are not paid by the hospital for those tests and procedures. Their revenue is generated when they see patients in their offices and for the performance of procedures they do in the hospital or in other clinical settings.

The relationship between doctors and hospitals has been both a cause of angst and a driver of collaboration between the two entities for decades:

angst because each has power over the other. The doctor needs the hospital in order to practice medicine, and the hospital needs the doctor to perform procedures and medical services and cannot earn patient services revenue without the doctor. Whether the doctor is on the payroll of the hospital or is in private practice, the hospital is reliant on the doctor for its revenue. It can only perform tests and procedures when a doctor orders them. Only licensed physicians may legally make medical decisions. Doctors, whether in private practice or employed by the hospital maintain independence in their medical decisions. The hospital's management exert their authority in the hospital organization through medical staff membership and quality control measures. These measures are related primarily to clinical care, care coordination, patient safety, and the patient/caregiver experience.

The medically related relationship between hospitals and physicians occurs through the mechanism of the medical staff. The medical staff organizationally gets its authority from the Board of Directors of the hospital. The board creates and empowers a formally structured Medical Staff organization composed of physicians who are members of the hospital staff and maintains a role in the functioning of the medical staff through medical staff bylaws and committee structure. The medical staff bylaws govern all aspects of a physician's hospital practice. To support coordination and collaboration between the hospital and its medical staff, a "Joint Conference Committee" is structured to bring together representatives from the board, hospital management and physicians to address management concerns, policies, strategies, and budgets. Other medical staff committees are also formed with specific areas of responsibility. These include the Credentials Committee, Utilization Review Committee, and Infection Control Committee. The medical staff functions in the pattern of hierarchical organizations with a chief of staff who is a practicing physician, an executive committee, and chairs of various specialties or departments of the hospital (e.g., surgery, orthopedics, pediatrics, gastroenterology). On a day-to-day basis, the chief of staff interacts closely with the president and CEO of the hospital, and it is these two who must forge a working relationship if the hospital is to be successful.

In order to practice in a hospital, it is required that physicians be admitted to the hospital Medical Staff through which they gain access to use of the facilities of the hospital for patient admissions, tests, and surgical and other procedures. The hospital is at risk for what happens in its facilities, and so maintains a stringent process through which physicians must be "credentialed" in order to gain medical staff membership. The physician applies to the Medical Staff for membership, and the Medical Staff follows a credentialing process that has been developed by it and approved by the hospital's Board of Directors. The application for membership is initially reviewed and approved by the Credentials Committee and is then submitted to the Executive Committee of the Medical Staff for approval. With that approval, and its subsequent acceptance by the hospital board, the physician becomes part of the medical staff and is authorized to admit patients, order tests, and treat or perform procedures on patients within the limits of the credentials he or she holds. The orthopedist, for example, is authorized to use hospital facilities and services for his or her patients within the range of approval given for his or her specialty and credentials.

The process for gaining and retaining hospital credentials is one in which the Medical Staff looks at all aspects of the physician's educational and practice experience and history. The committee reviews not only academic and practice credentials but also any history of malpractice or actions taken by other healthcare providers or within the legal system against the applicant physician.

While the hospital-physician relationship has been built on a structural model that has inherent tensions, the hospital-medical staff relationship is changing as healthcare and payment systems become more complex. As William Petasnick says in writing for *Frontiers of Health Services Management*:

> The old model . . . governed by the rules of the organized medical staff structure, doesn't work in the current environment, which has grown increasingly complex as a result of legal, economic, and care delivery changes. These complexities make relationship management challenging. Hospitals and physicians struggle to align behavior to achieve cost and quality goals. The need has never been greater for hospitals and physicians to work together as a joint clinical enterprise to improve quality, reduce practice variation, and control the cost of healthcare.
>
> (13)

4.4.2 Integrated Delivery Networks (IDNs)

An integrated delivery network (IDN) is a healthcare system that seeks to create a comprehensive integration of providers of care delivery in its target market area. IDNs were initially developed in the 1990s with the proliferation of managed care. As managed care payers structured their business model around achieving negotiated discount rates from healthcare providers, they also implemented a mechanism in which a case manager worked with the provider to ensure that services were used efficiently and not to excess in order to achieve acceptable rates of quality and cost reductions. Managed care companies approach hospitals and physicians with large numbers of enrolled members (employees and families insured by major employers) to seek volume discounts. Hospitals and physicians recognize the value of size at the negotiating table. If they do not strike a deal with the managed care company, they can be cut out of being included on the managed care company's panel of approved providers. When managed care companies formed and began this negotiating process, larger hospitals began to aggressively pursue acquisition of physician practices, ambulatory care, and surgical centers, and of other providers and hospitals. Size would give them the ability to control prices and aggregate services for overall reductions in cost and to reduce duplication of expensive services in the geographic area. It would also give them both presence in, and access to, primary and secondary markets of patients in their targeted market and would support the continuum of care in which all needed clinical services would be offered within the single organizational entity. In some cases, where acquisition or merger is not possible, contractual affiliations with other providers are created to achieve similar purposes.

There are approximately 413 hospital systems in the U.S. and these 413 systems include over 3,700 of the 6,090 registered hospitals in the U.S. Some of the hospitals not included in healthcare systems are those that are operated by the VA and by state and county authorities.

As IDNs create their structures in order to provide a continuum of care for the patient, they are reliant on the sophisticated information technology that is fundamental to full integration. Without the information infrastructure to support complete sharing of information between and among all the entities in the IDN, costs are duplicated, tests are duplicated, information is duplicated, and often one provider of care does not know what another has prescribed or tested for any given patient. Investment of billions of dollars in healthcare information technology (electronic health record or EHR) has been made by the federal government over the last decade and has achieved almost total adoption of EHRs by healthcare providers, yet most of these EHRs record and share information within the individual healthcare system, not with other healthcare systems. This means that if patients move among different systems, their medical records are still shared in cumbersome fashion (e.g., by fax). The fully shared EHR holds the promise of enabling sharing for improved decision making when the clinician comes face to face with the patient in whatever venue of care they find themselves, which is particularly important in emergency situations.

4.5 Summary

In this chapter, we discussed the major organizational structures in which healthcare providers organize themselves. Whether they are for-profits or not-for-profits, tax-exempt or taxed, each is a vital part of its community. The efforts to integrate multiple hospitals, nursing care facilities, rehabilitation, ambulatory care, physician practices, and other providers into one organizational entity are ongoing. In the current financial and reimbursement system, the individual provider is hard pressed to "stand alone," whether that is a physician practice, a small hospital, or a surgery center. Each is reliant on a system of referrals and on the sharing of administrative services and of high-priced medical and information technology. As the country faces shortages of primary care doctors and nurses, disparities in access to care, the demand for continuous quality improvement and reduction in the rate of cost increases, collaboration among hospitals, doctors, payers, and patients is critical.

References

1. C. Evashwick. 1989 (Spring). Creating the continuum of care. *Health Matrix*, 7(1): 30–39. PMID: 10293297. Available at https://pubmed.ncbi.nlm.nih.gov/10293297/.
2. C.J. Evashwick. 1989 (June). Creating a continuum: The goal is to provide an integrated system of care. *Health Progress*, 70(5): 36–39. PMID: 10293328. Available at https://pubmed.ncbi.nlm.nih.gov/10293328/.
3. J. Henry, Y. Pylypchuk, et al. 2016 (May). Adoption of electronic health record systems among U.S. non-federal acute care hospitals: 2008–2015. *ONC Data Brief 35*. Available at https://dashboard.healthit.gov/evaluations/data-briefs/non-federal-acute-care-hospital-ehr-adoption-2008-2015.php.
4. Department of Veterans Affairs. *Providing health care for veterans*. Available at www.va.gov/health/. Last updated April 8, 2021.
5. Indian Health Services. *About IHS*. Available at www.ihs.gov/newsroom/factsheets/ihsprofile/.
6. J. James. 2016 (Feb. 25). Health policy brief: Nonprofit hospitals' community benefit requirements. *Health Affairs*. Available at www.healthaffairs.org/do/10.1377/hpb20160225.954803/full/.

7. J. Carlson. 2008 (Oct. 20). Unlocking the community chest. *Modern Healthcare*, 38(42): 6–7, 16, 1. PMID: 18975415.

8. Rural Health Information Hub (RHIhub). *Critical access hospitals.* Available at www.ruralhealthinfo.org/topics/critical-access-hospitals#:~:text=The%20 Flex%20Monitoring%20Team%20maintains%20a%20list%20of,of%20Critical%20 Access%20Hospitals%20across%20the%20United%20States.

9. NIH. U.S. National Library of Medicine. *Regional medical programs: A brief history.* Available at https://profiles.nlm.nih.gov/spotlight/rm/feature/brief history.

10 Association of American Medical Schools (AAMC). 2019 (July 25). *U.S. medical school enrollment surpasses expansion goal.* Available at www.aamc.org/news-insights/ press-releases/us-medical-school-enrollment-surpasses-expansion-goal.

11. Statista. *Number of psychiatric hospitals in the U.S. in 2019 by operation type.* Available at www.statista.com/statistics/712645/psychiatric-hospitals-number-in-the-us-by-operation-type/.

12. T.A. Henry. 2019 (May 10). Employed physicians now exceed those who own practices. *American Medical Association.* Available at www.ama-assn.org/ about/research/employed-physicians-now-exceed-those-who-own-their-practices.

13. W.D. Petasnick. 2007. Hospital-physician relationships: Imperative for clinical enterprise collaboration. *Frontiers of Health Services Management*, 24(1): 3.

Chapter 5

Doctors

5.1 Introduction

Historically, and still today, physicians and hospitals have a special relation-ship. As discussed in Chapter 4, they are completely interdependent, yet they work under different business models. The way in which physicians are integrated into healthcare delivery is changing as they take on new and expanding roles. While for more than half a century physicians have worked almost exclusively in their own private practices, holding medical staff privileges at local hospitals for inpatient admissions and testing, they currently are in management roles in increasing numbers and on hospital payrolls working as hospitalists, as intensivists, and in other clinical areas. Many have also sold their practice to a local hospital or a Physician Practice Management Organization in which they may have ownership and are on the payroll of their new employer. There are approximately one million physicians in clinical practice, management, research, and other roles in the United States.

5.2 Physician Workforce

Of the approximately one million licensed physicians in the United States, 938,980 were actively practicing medicine in 2018 according to the Association of American Medical Colleges (AAMC). (1) According to 2019 data from the AAMC, just over 350,000 licensed U.S. physicians are in the primary care specialties of general internal medicine, family medicine, pediatrics, internal medicine-pediatrics, and obstetrics/gynecology. The balance of physicians in 2019 practiced in other specialties (see Table 5.1). The United States continues to face a significant shortage of primary care physicians to serve the increasing demand for primary care as driven by payers and consumers and, particularly by the needs of an aging baby boomer population. The AAMC issued a report in July of 2020 estimating a shortage of 21,400 to 55,200 primary care physicians by 2033. The AAMC report goes on to estimate a shortage of 54,100 to 139,000 of the combined specialty and primary care physicians in the same time frame. (2)

The average annual income for primary care physicians is lower than that for most other specialties. This creates a disincentive for medical students to choose a primary care field. For example, the Bureau of Labor Statistics (BLS) reported in April of 2021 that the median income for anesthesiologists was $271,440 and that for surgeons was $251,650. In contrast, family practitioners earned a median income of $214,370 and general internists

Table 5.1   Number of Physicians in Selected Specialties, 2019

Anesthesiology	42,267
Cardiovascular Disease	22,521
Dermatology	12,516
Emergency Medicine	45,202
General Surgery	25,042
Infectious Disease	9,687
Internal Medicine	120,171
Obstetrics and Gynecology	42,720
Orthopedic Surgery	19,069
Pediatrics	60,618
Psychiatry	38,792
Radiation Oncology	5,306

Source: Association of American Medical Colleges. 2019 (Dec.). Number of people per active physician by specialty, 2019. Available at www.aamc.org/what-we-do/mission-areas/health-care/workforce-studies/interactive-data/number-people-active-physician-specialty-2019

Table 5.2   Median Income for Physicians, May 2020

Anesthesiologists	$271,440
Surgeons	251,650
Obstetricians and gynecologists	239,120
Psychiatrists	217,100
Family and general practitioners	214,370
Internists, general	210,960
Pediatricians, general	184,570

Source: Bureau of Labor Statistics. Last modified April 9, 2021. Occupational outlook handbook, physicians and surgeons, pay. Available at www.bls.gov/ooh/healthcare/physicians-and-surgeons.htm#tab-5

earned a $210,960 median income (see Table 5.2). Yet, from national mortality perspective, a study published in the Journal of the American Medical Association in 2019 reported that "every 10 additional primary care physicians per 100,000 population was associated with a 51.5 day increase in life expectancy. However, from 2005 to 2015, the density of primary care physicians decreased from 46.6 to 41.4 per 100,000." (3)

5.3 Physician Education

Medical schools are organized within one of two medical disciplines: allopathy and osteopathy. Allopathy is defined as "a philosophy of medicine that views medical treatment as active intervention to counteract the effects of disease through medical and surgical procedures that produce effects opposite to those of the disease" (4) or as a "therapeutic system in which a disease is treated by producing a second condition that is incompatible with or antagonistic to the first." (5) Osteopathy on the other hand is a medical philosophy based on the holistic approach to treatment. It uses the traditional methods of medical practice, which includes pharmaceuticals, laboratory tests, X-ray diagnostics, and surgery, and supplements them by advocating treatment that involves correction of the position of the joints or tissues and by emphasizing diet and environment as factors that might destroy natural resistance. (4)

Even though allopathic and osteopathic physicians are trained in different philosophical approaches to disease and healing, both complete similar rigorous didactic and clinical training and both are required to pass the licensure examination in order to practice medicine in the United States.

5.3.1 Medical School

Today there are 155 allopathic medical school programs and 48 osteopathic medical college programs leading to the MD or DO degree in the United States. Enrollment in these programs was at a total of just over 88,000 medical students in the 2016–2017 academic year. By 2020–2021, enrollments had increased to just over 94,000 (Table 5.3). It is significant to note that the number of female enrollees outpaced males during this time period. In 2016–2017, 42,036 women were enrolled compared to 46,149 men. By 2020–2021, the numbers had reversed to about 48,530 women and 45,675 men (Table 5.3).

Enrollment in medical schools in the U.S. had been relatively static prior to 2000. However, calls for expansion of capacity in order to meet a forecast burgeoning need for physicians resulted in an unusually rapid expansion of capacity through increases in class sizes but primarily through the establishment of new medical schools throughout the U.S. By 2019, 29 new accredited medical schools and 17 new schools of osteopathic medicine had been opened. The expansion of medical school capacity was a significant step toward addressing the issue of physician shortages in the U.S., however residency slots for specialist and primary care training needed to be expanded to keep up the pace for physician training.

Residency training programs are federally funded through Medicare and were capped by Congress for decades. Thus, limited residency opportunities were available for medical school graduates for decades. In mid-2019, the

Table 5.3   Medical School Enrollments: 2016–2017 & 2020–2021

U.S. Medical School Enrollments			
	Men	*Women*	*All*
Year			
2016–2017	46,149	42,036	88,185
2020–2021	45,675	48,530	92,243

Source: American Association of Medical Colleges. 2020 (Nov. 3). Medical school enrollments. Available at www.aamc.org/media/6101/download

government announced that $20 million in grants from the Health Resources and Services Administration (HRSA) would be provided for 27 U.S. healthcare provider organizations to set up new residency programs to train additional doctors for work in rural areas. (6) Subsequently, in 2021, in order to further expand residency opportunities, CMS announced that "as part of the fiscal 2022 'inpatient prospective payment system,' 1,000 new Medicare-funded physician residency slots will be distributed to qualifying hospitals." (7)

5.3.2 Typical Course of Study in Medical School

The typical medical school curriculum is broken down into two parts and designed around the progression of the student through the education program. Entering students are required to have a premedical undergraduate education grounded in the sciences. Following graduation from college, they then enroll in a four-year medical school program. In the first and second years of medical school, students are primarily in the classroom studying basic sciences; the third and fourth years are spent primarily out of the classroom and in the clinical setting gaining experience in working with inpatients and with outpatients in teaching hospitals or academic medical centers. In some instances, students enroll in a six- to eight-year program that integrates both undergraduate and medical school programs.

5.3.2.1 Preclinical Curriculum

Once they are enrolled in medical school, the first two years are often called the "preclinical" phase of their education. Although students have clinical experience throughout medical school, the two-year preclinical phase occurs in the classroom with didactic learning. The basic science departments of the school are largely responsible for the content of the preclinical curriculum. Here, the normal structure and function of human systems are taught through gross and microscopic anatomy, biochemistry, physiology, behavioral science, and neuroscience. After students' completion of the basic sciences, the educational focus shifts to abnormalities of the body's structure and function, disease, and general therapeutic principles through courses in microbiology, immunology, pharmacology, and pathology.

After the second year of medical school, students take the first of a series of national exams required of medical students, the United States Medical Licensing Examination (USMLE). Passing the first USMLE is required to continue in medical school.

5.3.2.2 Clinical Phase of Medical Education

Having successfully completed step one of the USMLE, the student moves into the third year of medical school. The clinical phase of the curriculum is devoted primarily to education in the clinical setting. These periods of instruction are called clerkships, and they may range in length from approximately four to 12 weeks. During clerkships, students work with patients and their families in inpatient and outpatient settings.

Required "core" clerkships in all schools include internal medicine, pediatrics, psychiatry, surgery, obstetrics/gynecology, and family medicine. Depending on the school, required clerkships can also include other specialties such as family medicine, primary care, neurology, and community or rural medicine.

While in a hospital setting or a hospital clinic, students work under the supervision of physician faculty members (known as "attending physicians") and physician residents, and they work with other members of the health-care team, including nurses, social workers, psychologists, pharmacists, and other technical staff. Following completion of medical school, the graduate physician completes a one-year internship in their chosen specialty. This internship may be the first year of a residency program if they pursue a residency.

5.3.3 Medical Licensing

The USMLE transitioned from a three-phase to a two-phase exam process that must be successfully completed sequentially during and after medical school. After successful completion, the physician can apply for licensure in the state in which he/she wants to practice medicine.

Individual states are responsible for the licensing of physicians, and in doing so their requirements will vary depending on state legislation and on the unique requirements of the state. Upon receipt of the state medical license, the newly minted physician can go on to practice general medicine. The physician who decides to practice in another state, is required to be licensed in that state. If the state is among the 30 states who participate in the Interstate Medical Licensure Compact (IMLC), the licensure process can be expedited through reciprocity agreements. (8)

For the newly licensed physician, the typical progression is to continue their education in a medical residency in a specialty in which they intend to practice (e.g., orthopedics, otolaryngology, pediatrics, surgery, family practice). The residency is designed to prepare the physician for Board Certification in their chosen specialty.

5.3.4 Preparation of the Specialist

Residencies are offered at teaching hospitals and academic medical centers. The physician faculty in these institutions combine both an active medical office practice in a "faculty practice plan" and devote time to supervising the training of residents within the specific specialties for which they and the hospital or medical center are approved. Residencies for medical specialization last from three to five years, depending on the specialty chosen; if the physician then decides to pursue a sub-specialty (e.g., retinal specialist is a sub-specialty of ophthalmology), he or she will spend another one to three years completing a *fellowship* in the sub-specialty.

Upon completion of the specialty residency, physicians must successfully complete an examination given by their respective specialty board. The American Board of Medical Specialties is the overarching body for the 24 specialty Boards that are members. Together, they represent 40 specialties and 87 subspecialties.

Finally, having completed a specialty and/or sub-specialty, board-certified physicians are required to maintain that certification through the Maintenance of Certification (MOC) of the American Board of Medical Specialties. The Maintenance of Certification requires ongoing medical education so that the physician can maintain skills and stay abreast of advances in the field and periodic assessments or examinations in which they must demonstrate continuing and up-to-date skill in the specialty. The requirements for continuing medical education may vary by state.

5.4 International Medical Graduates

In 2020 the United States admitted 7,376 international medical graduates (IMGs) to residencies in the country. Of these, about 3,154 were U.S. IMGs (i.e., U.S. citizens who started medical school in other countries) and about 4,222 were non-U.S. IMGs (i.e., medical school graduates who are not U.S. citizens but who are certified to enter a residency or fellowship in the United States; see Table 5.4). Certification by the Educational Commission for Foreign Medical Graduates (ECFMG) is required of all IMGs to enter a residency in the United States. In order to be certified for a residency match

Table 5.4   International Medical Graduates Entering U.S. Residency Programs

Entry Year	Applicants	Total Matched	U.S. IMGs Matched	Non-U.S. IMGs Matched
2019	11,949	7,025	2,997	4,028
2020	12,074	7,376	3,154	4,222

Source: Educational Commission for Foreign Medical Graduates. International Medical Graduate (IMG) performance in the 2020 main residency match. Available at www.ecfmg.org/resources/Match2020Infographic.pdf and at www.ecfmg.org/news/2019/03/15/imgs-continue-to-show-gains-in-2019-match/

in which the graduate physician applicant requests an appropriate residency assignment to the specialty in which they want to practice, the IMG must pass the USMLE. Many IMGs requesting residencies in the United States enter primary care specialties–general internal medicine, family medicine and pediatrics in that order of preference.

5.5 Financial Support of Medical Education

Historically, medical schools have relied on a number of revenue sources. The clinical practice of faculty has been a significant source of funding–up to one-third of total medical school income is generated by the faculty from the patient care they deliver in the Faculty Practice Plan (i.e., a "group practice" in which they have scheduled office hours to see patients). Student tuition, research grants and contracts provide for a portion of funding requirements and another portion of support is derived from endowments. Much of the balance of funding comes from Medicare's subsidization of graduate medical education (GME). However, that support has been gradually diminishing, and this scaling back of subsidies for GME has reduced revenues for academic medical centers and teaching hospitals. Additionally, academic medical centers (AMCs) tend to be more expensive than other hospitals because of the numbers of charity patients they serve and the complex cases, trauma and burn victims to whom they provide services. In addition, the cost of medical education and the availability of state-of-the-art technologies in medical training specialties add to the costs of AMCs. In this era of increasing financial pressure on hospitals, there is strong pressure on teaching hospitals and medical schools to find other means of support for medical education.

According to the AAMC, first year tuition in a public medical school averaged $37,556 in 2019–2020 and in a private school the average was $60,665. (9)

5.6 The Physician–Hospital Relationship

As discussed in Chapter 4, doctors are credentialed by, and admitted to, membership on the medical staff of a hospital prior to being permitted to perform procedures or admit patients to the hospital. The medical staff, which is a formally organized body under the authority of the hospital's board of directors, is the physicians' organizational structure in the hospital.

In a separate arrangement, certain specialist physician groups are contracted by the hospital to provide core services that the hospital provides. The services that are typically staffed by contract physicians include radiology (X-ray), pathology (lab), anesthesia, and the emergency department.

Contract physicians do not admit patients to the hospital. While emergency physicians provide urgent care to emergency department (ED) patients, they also do not admit patients for inpatient care. When patients need to be admitted, they are referred to an admitting physician in the hospital. The emergency physician does not provide ongoing care to admitted patients.

Often, a contract specialist physician serves as the medical head or director of their respective department. They also provide specialized services to support the diagnosis and treatment of patients and are paid under contractual arrangements. They do not receive a salary from the hospital but bill the hospitals for their role in reading and reporting test results (e.g., an X-ray) or in providing certain treatments.

In many cases, hospitals hire primary care physicians who work in an office practice in the geographical service area of the hospital where they see patients in their offices. The office-based physicians are paid a salary by the hospital and their staffing and business office functions are provided by the hospital. The number of employed primary care physicians continues to grow as hospitals expand their networks geographically and provide essential services in selected markets, to manage the quality and costs of care, and to stabilize the scope of their services. For office-based physicians, the lower salary they might receive as an employee of the hospital is a welcome tradeoff from having to work long office hours in private practice. They are happy to gain an improved work-life balance and to be removed from the demands of managing an office, the complexities of health insurance systems, increasing revenue pressures from government and private payers, and increasing costs of doing business

The traditional role of physicians in hospitals and that of the medical staff structure are under ongoing review and change to meet the needs of a changing healthcare system, scientific advances, and patient expectations. Physicians are increasingly moving into newly defined roles within the hospital. *Hospitalists* are physicians who are hired or contracted by the hospital to provide in-patient medical care to patients who are admitted to the hospitals and often are the admitting doctor and/or "attending of record" for patients referred from the emergency room or from primary care physicians. Hospitalists work in the inpatient units of the hospital, and, in larger health systems, specialists may fill these roles in the specialty inpatient units of the health system. For example, intensivists work specifically in the intensive care and cardiac care units. In both instances, when a patient's doctor admits him or her, that patient's in-hospital care is provided by the hospitalist unless specialty services are required (e.g., orthopedic surgery). This works particularly well for primary care physicians and certain specialists who would otherwise be required to share 24/7 coverage of their hospitalized inpatients (i.e., be on call at scheduled hours of the day, night, and weekends). Hospitalists are paid a salary by the hospital and are scheduled to work regular staff hours.

The number of physicians in *management roles* is increasing in hospitals. Physicians historically managed hospitals, but with the introduction of the healthcare management profession in the mid-twentieth century in the U.S. and the establishment of graduate programs in healthcare management, the role evolved into a business model and became populated by non-physician professionals. There has been a shift in many healthcare systems back to engaging physicians in management roles. In these roles, the physician typically spends little time in the direct care of patients and instead is responsible for the management of resources, for interrelationships, and for other leadership, strategic, and administrative duties. In hospital management, physicians are often employed in upper management roles such as:

■ Chief Executive Officer or CEO
■ Chief Medical officer or CMO
■ Chief Information Officer or CIO
■ Chief Medical Information Officer or CMIO
■ Other related roles

Many doctors who admit patients to the hospital and perform surgery or other procedures are not employees of the hospital–the hospital does not pay them a salary. While some doctors are hired by the hospital to work as hospitalists and others are hired to work in the management of the hospital as described earlier, most specialty physicians are not employed or paid by the hospital. Neither does the hospital bill the insurance company on behalf of the doctor. That leaves the doctor to do his or her own billing for services. In order to navigate the complexities of regulatory and payer requirements, many physicians today are owners in, or employed by, larger physician practices, many under the structure of a Physician Practice Management Organization.

For doctors who are not employed by a hospital, income is generated from their clinical care of patients in the office and from procedures performed in the hospital or outpatient setting (e.g., surgery, deliveries). The physician bills insurers for clinical visits to patients in hospitals and for treatments or procedures performed in hospitals and ambulatory centers. If, for example, a dermatologist performs an outpatient surgical procedure in an ambulatory center, then that dermatologist directly bills the patient's insurer or health plan for the physician's role in that procedure and the ambulatory center bill the insurer for the fees related to the use of the facility and supplies and staff costs. The complexity of payer pricing and billing practices has motivated many physicians to join group practices as described earlier.

The concept of balance billing is important, though it is becoming rarer. When the patient makes a visit to a physician or hospital that is not in the payer network of providers approved by his or her insurance, they may receive a separate bill for the full, non-discounted, fee. In this case, the provider is not bound by a payment agreement with the patient's insurer. While that insurer might pay the portion of the fee that is equal or near the amount that would be paid to an in-network provider, the balance between the full charge and the discounted payment is frequently charged to the patient. This may take the patient by surprise, especially when they, for example, go to an emergency room and do not know that, while the hospital's ER is in-network, the ER physician may not be, or when they are admitted for a surgical procedure and are not aware that the anesthesiologist is not in-network. Increasingly, states are taking action to make this practice illegal.

5.7 Malpractice

While Chapter 7 addresses some of the public policy actions that have been taken to address the crisis in malpractice that the United States has faced, it is appropriate to discuss the topic briefly here. Malpractice has frequently been the subject of heated and intense discussion. This comes from two perspectives.

On the one hand, many physicians pay very high premiums (some say dispro-portionately high) for their malpractice insurance, particularly in certain special-ties such as obstetrics/gynecology or because of their geographic location. This may be a dis-incentive for physicians to choose those specialties or geographic areas in which to live. On the other hand, patients who are injured in a medical error or through negligence often feel that they deserve to be financially "made whole" and/or to be assured that the same error is not repeated. They may turn to litigation in this situation. The American Medical Association (AMA) reported in 2018 that "more than one in three physicians, 34%, have had a medical liabil-ity lawsuit filed against them at some point in their career." (10)

Medical malpractice insurance is expensive, especially for certain special-ties. On average, medical malpractice insurance costs about $7,500 annually, according to Physicians Thrive Investment Advisors. For surgeons, annual premiums can range between $30,000 and $50,000 and up depending on their location. For OB/GYNs, premiums can cost in the hundreds of thou-sands of dollars, again, based on location. (11)

The National Practitioner Data Bank (NPDB) was created by the U.S. Congress as one initiative to address the growing crisis in medical malprac-tice litigation and to improve quality of care in the United States. The NPDB is a web-based repository that functions under the auspices of the Health Resources and Services Agency (HRSA) in the Department of Health and Human Services (HHS). It receives reports of malpractice payments and adverse actions concerning healthcare practitioners. Adverse actions are those taken against physicians subsequent to a finding of error or wrong-doing on their part. The adverse actions may be related to their licensure, clinical privileges, professional society membership, and participation in Medicare and Medicaid. When adverse actions are taken, that information is reported to the NPDB and then made available to approved entities for review when considering an action relative to an individual physician, such as the granting of medical staff privileges to admit and treat patients in a hospital. It is essentially an alert or flagging system meant to support com-prehensive reviews of physicians. It is however confidential, and only autho-rized entities can gain access to it. It is not available to the public.

5.8 Summary

The role of physicians in healthcare is complex. Functioning as independent practitioners, they are integrally tied to hospitals and healthcare systems. The mutual interdependency of hospitals and doctors has long been a source of angst and has resulted in continually evolving roles and adaptation. Professionals who work among hospitals and doctors, need to understand this relationship, its challenges, and its impact on the delivery of medical care. Looking to the future, the United States is facing a substantial shortage of physicians, particularly physicians in primary care specialties. This need will drive a further expansion of medical education and of opportunities to provide primary care (e.g., through nurse practitioners and physician assistants). In all, the way in which this expansion is financed will determine if the U.S. will be able to meet the needs of a growing population

References

1. American Association of Medical Colleges. 2020. *Number of people per active physician by specialty, 2019.* Available at www.aamc.org/what-we-do/mission-areas/health-care/workforce-studies/interactive-data/number-people-active-physician-specialty-2019.
2. Primary Care Collaborative of the American Association of Medical Colleges. 2020. *The complexities of physician supply and demand projections from 2018–2033.* Available at www.pcpcc.org/2020/07/10/new-report-confirms-growing-shortage-primary-care-physicians#:~:text=July%2010%2C%20 2020.%20Association%20of%20American%20Medical%20Colleges.,and-%20139%2C000%20of%20all%20physicians%20%28primary%20and%20 specialty%29.
3. S. Basu, S.A. Berkowitz, R.L. Phillips, et al. 2019 (Feb. 8). Association of primary care physician supply with population mortality in the United States, 2005–2015. *JAMA Internal Medicine,* 179(4): 506–514. doi:10.1001/jamainternmed.2018.7624.
4. L. Shi and D.A. Singh. 2001. *Delivering health care in America: A systems approach.* Gaithersburg, MD: Aspen Publishers, p. 581.
5. American Association of Colleges of Osteopathic Medicine. 2006. *Educational Council on Osteopathic Principles (ECOP) of the glossary of osteopathic terminology usage guide.* Available at www.osteopathic.org.
6. J. Finnegan. 2019 (July 16). More medical students than ever, but more residency slots needed to solve physician shortage, AAMC says. *Fierce Healthcare.* Available at www.fiercehealthcare.com/practices/more-medical-students-than-ever-but-more-residency-slots-needed-to-solve-physician.
7. B. Japsen. 2021 (December 17). To address doctor shortage, U.S. to pay for 1,000 new residencies. *Forbes.* Available at https://www.forbes.com/sites/brucejapsen/2021/12/17/to-address-urban-and-rural-doctor-shortage-us-to-pay-for-1000-new-residencies/?sh=52eaa0e8a7b6#:~:text=Under%20 a%20rule%20implemented%20by%20the%20Centers%20for,five%20 years%2C%E2%80%9D%20CMS%20said%20Friday%20in%20an%20 announcement.

8. A. Robeznieks. 2021 (Apr. 26). Cross-state licensing process now live in 30 states. *American Medical Association.* Available at www.ama-assn. org/news-leadership-viewpoints/authors-news-leadership-viewpoints/ andis-robeznieks.

9. R. Lake. 2021 (Mar. 28). *The average cost of medical school.* Available at www. thebalance.com/average-cost-of-medical-school-4588236#:~:text=According%20 to%20the%20Association%20of%20American%20Medical%20 Colleges,private%20medical%20school%20paid%20even%20more%2C%20at%20 %2460%2C665.

10. K.B. O'Reilly. 2018 (Jan. 26). 1 in 3 physicians has been sued; by age 55, 1 in 2 hit with suit. *American Medical Association.* Available at www.ama-assn.org/ practice-management/sustainability/1-3-physicians-has-been-sued-age-55-1-2-hit-suit. Accessed May 10, 2021.

11. Physicians Thrive. *How much does malpractice insurance cost?* Available at https://physiciansthrive.com/financial-planning/malpractice-insurance-cost/. Accessed May 10, 2021.

Chapter 6

The Healthcare Workforce

6.1 Introduction

The healthcare provider workforce is composed of a widely varying array of professional clinical specialties, support staff, and administrative and support personnel. These professionals and staff work not only in hospitals but also in nursing homes, home health agencies, physician offices, clinics, pharmacies, emergency services, hospice programs, ambulatory centers, diagnostic labs, and other settings. Concurrent to the growth of the healthcare provider sector, the demand for trained allied health clinicians (a broad term that includes nurses, laboratory and radiology technologists, pharmacists, therapists, dietitians, and other licensed clinicians) has grown and continues to grow.

6.2 Nursing

Nursing is by far the largest single profession in the healthcare provider system's workforce. Nursing may comprise up to 50 percent of that workforce in a hospital system. Similar to physicians on the medical staff, nurses work in any of a number of clinical departments in the hospital, and many become specialized in their clinical area of choice–pediatrics, emergency services, surgery, obstetrics, and so on. They also function at various levels of training and certification or licensure including Advanced Practice Nurses (APN), Registered Nurses (RN), and licensed practical nurses or licensed vocational nurses (LPN/LVN).

DOI: 10.4324/9781003202950-6

The Lippincott Nursing Center, referencing data from a 2018 national survey conducted by the U.S. Department of Health and Human Services, Health Resources and Services Administration, reported in May, 2020 that

- the average age of nurses is 48–50
- nearly half of all nurses are over the age of 50
- there is a growing number of male nurses who in 2018 comprised 9.6 percent of the nursing workforce
- 26.7 percent of nurses were minorities in 2018
- the median salary for nurses was $73,300/year.

(1)

Figure 6.1 depicts the major sectors of healthcare in which RNs worked in the 2018. Fully 60 percent of RNs worked in hospitals, 18 percent in ambulatory services, and 7 percent in nursing and residential facilities. About 8 percent of RNs worked in other settings. These include other healthcare delivery venues, governmental services, and educational programs. (2)

Within the hospital organization, nurses work as salaried or hourly staff. They report within the organizational structure of the nursing department in the health system. Nurses typically function in different clinical nursing roles, for example, as unit nurses, specialists, or as a charge nurse in inpatient or outpatient units. They may also transition into nursing management

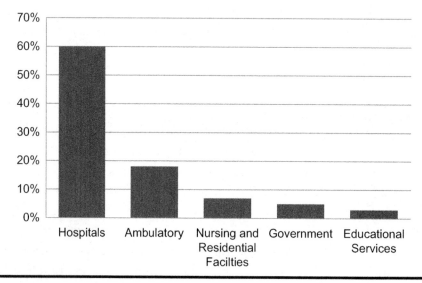

Figure 6.1 Where Nurses Work

Source: M.B. Schnur, MSN, RN. 2020 (May 28). U.S. Nurses in 2020: Who we are and where we work. Lippicott Nursing Center. Available at https://www.nursing center.com/ncblog/may-2020/u-s-nurses-in-2020.

roles and advance hierarchically up to a director or vice president of nursing and to the C-suite.

Nursing departments are staffed around the clock and work in a "matrix" type of arrangement in which physicians write orders for clinical services and procedures that are to be done for patients, and nurses and other clinical staff carry out those orders. Nurses also are empowered to make patient care decisions within the scope of their clinical protocols. When nurses move into management functions they assume responsibility for operational effectiveness and efficiency in the nursing department. Duties may include ensuring that adequate and qualified nurses are hired, scheduled, and receive continuing education to maintain their license, that patient care protocols are adopted and practiced consistently, that budgets are met, that clinical and process quality mechanisms are in place and followed, and that nursing and patient care goals and objectives are met.

Just as the relationship between physicians and hospital management is critical for the reasons discussed in Chapter 5, the relationship between nurses and physicians is also of vital importance. While nurses are required to follow the orders of doctors, they also have the unique and challenging role of bringing their training and experience to situational decision-making. They constantly observe patients' progress and responses to medications and treatments and, in urgent situations, make and act on decisions that are within nursing practice protocols. Patients' lives and well-being are in their hands and so nurses make life-saving and life-sustaining decisions frequently.

There are three professional categories of licensure for nurses. These include: Advanced Practice Registered Nurse (APRN), Registered Nurse (RN), and Licensed Practical Nurse (LPN). One additional designation for nurses is the Certified Nurse Assistant (CNA) which requires certification but not licensure. The following discussion addresses the licensed nursing categories. Registered Nurses are the largest demographic among nurses.

6.2.1 Registered Nurses

RNs have professional opportunities in a wide array of settings and functions. Those roles include, among others, direct patient care in the clinical setting, organizational management, information technology, operational management, research, education, the legal profession, and others.

Of these roles, the majority of RNs work in the clinical setting providing direct patient care. Here the RN is responsible for assessment of patients using their training, experience, and clinical judgment to perform nursing diagnosis, treatment, and evaluation of the progress of the patient and the effectiveness of patient care. The nurse plays a key role in the nursing team that designs and implements the care plan for each patient according to that patient's condition. The clinical areas in which RNs work include, among others:

- Ambulatory care
- Hospitals–all clinical departments
- Surgery
- Critical, intensive, and neonatal care
- Emergency, trauma, and transport
- Home healthcare
- Hospice and palliative care
- Long-term care
- Physician offices
- Psychiatric–mental health services
- Rehabilitation
- Others

There is a uniquely structured set of alternative educational paths by which an individual can pursue his or her nursing education. According to the American Nurses Association, an individual aspiring to become an RN can acquire a bachelor's degree in nursing (BSN), a diploma in nursing (DIP), or an associate degree in nursing (ADN). In 2018, 1,035 U.S. colleges and universities offered the BSN or an advanced nursing degree. Enrollment in these programs in 2020 totaled 251,145. (3) The course of study for BSNs, DIPs and ADNs are different in several ways however they all must successfully complete the National Council Licensure Exam (NCLEX) in order to practice nursing. In the U.S. the potential courses of study for the RN are:

- The bachelors of science in nursing (BSN) requires four years of study. During those four years, students are provided both didactic studies in the classroom as well as clinical experience. Course work includes nursing theory, the sciences, humanities, and behavioral science preparation needed for the full scope of professional nursing responsibilities. The BSN also provides the background for advanced education that is required for an advanced practice nursing (APN) degree and for specialization in clinical practice and research. In 2019, 56 percent of all RNs were bachelor's prepared.

(4)

■ A diploma in nursing (DIN) requires up to three years of study. It combines classroom and clinical instruction and prepares the student for entry-level nursing positions. Diploma programs are hospital-based and, while they include substantial didactic learning, they place an emphasis on experiential clinical practice and patient care. Diploma nursing programs have diminished in number in the past couple of decades as nursing education has shifted from hospitals to academic institutions, and as hospitals have placed more emphasis on hiring BSN-prepared nurses.

■ An associate's degree in nursing (ADN) requires two years of study and prepares the nurse for an entry-level nursing position. The ADN prepares individuals for a defined technical scope of practice. These programs are typically offered by community colleges and vocational schools.

Because the BSN is a more demanding and longer course of study, nurses with BSNs tend to be in higher demand for job opportunities than do ADNs and diploma nurses and have a higher likelihood of professional advancement and increased clinical and management responsibility. In December 2020 AACN reported that, based on its survey titled *Employment of New Nurse Graduates and Preferences for Baccalaureate-Prepared Nurses*, "41.1% of hospitals and other healthcare settings are requiring new hires to have a bachelor's degree in nursing, while 82.4% of employers are expressing a strong preference for BSN program graduates." (5) The AACN report also notes that "A significant body of research shows that nurses with baccalaureate level preparation are linked to better patient outcomes, including lower mortality and failure-to-rescue rates." (5)

Upon graduation from a state-approved school of nursing, the aspiring RN must pass the NCLEX-RN to obtain a license to practice. The NCLEX is used for registered nurses in the U.S., Canada, and Australia. Continuing education or competency requirements to maintain RN licensure are established by state boards of nursing, which also handle disciplinary actions in the profession. Once licensed, the RN must practice in accordance with the requirements of the nurse practice act in the state in which he or she functions. RN licensure is reciprocal among many states that participate in the Nursing Licensure Compact (NLC), but the RN who wants to practice in another state must apply to that state's Board of Nursing in order to receive the reciprocal nursing license. This also applies to traveling nurses who accept temporary assignments in states other than the one in which they hold their original license to practice.

6.2.2 Advanced Practice Registered Nurses

Advanced practice nurses (APRNs or APNs), earn a master's degree in nursing and some go on to receive a doctor of nursing practice (DPN). Upon completion of their formal education, they are required to apply for licensure in the state in which they want to practice. The career of an APN may take one of several paths: nurse practitioner (NP), certified nurse midwive (CNM), certified registered nurse anesthetist (CRNA) or clinical nurse specialists (CNSs). Their primary roles are in the coordination of patient care and in providing primary and specialty healthcare clinical services. The field of nursing offers these clinicians the opportunity to train and work at varying levels of expertise or specialty such as pediatrics, family practice, and orthopedics. The Bureau of Labor Statistics, Occupational Employment and Wage Statistics reports that the median annual wage for advanced practice nurses in May 2020 was $111,680. Employment opportunities for APNs is strong and projected by the BLS "to grow 45 percent from 2019 to 2029". (6)

The role of each of the four specializations that are available to APNs are distinct. In each of these advanced nursing practices, the professional is required to complete certification in the area in which he/she decides to practice.

■ 6.3.3.1 Clinical Nurse Specialist (CNS)

– There are over 70,000 CNSs in the United States. CNSs may specialize in an area such as adult health or gerontology or pediatrics. They work primarily in hospitals providing care in areas such as cardiology, oncology, obstetrics/gynecology, pediatrics, neurology, and mental health. Others work in clinics, nursing homes, private offices, and community-based settings and, in many cases, serve in management roles relative to quality and performance improvement, best nursing practices, and evidence-based patient care. They may work in nursing informatics and other functions that support the nursing services in the healthcare system.

– CNSs also teach in nursing education programs. With the high demand for professional nurses, the need for nursing faculty is high and the lack of faculty is of particular concern because it is a barrier to expanding nurse training programs. Fang and Keston reported that "projected retirements in 2016–2025 would equal one third of faculty in 2015." (7) The looming retirement of nursing instructors accentuates the demand for increasing numbers of CNSs.

■ Nurse Practitioners (NPs)

- Nurse Practitioners (NPs) complete a master's degree in nursing. There are more than 325,000 NPs in the United States currently. They work in a variety of primary care and hospital services performing patient care functions such as physical exams, diagnosis and treatment of acute illnesses and injuries, immunizations, chronic disease management, patient education, and ordering/interpreting tests.

- NPs are authorized to prescribe medications in all 50 states, and they can practice independently without physician collaboration or supervision under "full practice" status in 22 states. They are often described as "physician extenders," particularly in that they may perform certain primary care services as they work in a specialist's office (e.g., taking patient histories, providing patient education, and following up on surgical procedures). They are authorized to diagnose common conditions and to prescribe drugs and treatments within a limited range in the primary care setting. NPs are authorized to bill directly for their services under certain governmental and private health insurer arrangements.

- The development and dramatic growth of mini-clinics over the past several decades have been possible through the employment of NPs who are often the sole clinical professional diagnosing and treating patients in this setting. Almost 90 percent of NPs are certified in primary care according to the Bureau of Labor Statistics. (8)

■ Nurse Midwives

- Nurse midwives (CNMs) are licensed by states to assist in obstetrical care and at the delivery of infants. This field of nursing has a long history as it developed out of a need for labor and delivery nurses in rural and underserved areas in the nineteenth and twentieth centuries. Financially, nurse midwives invoice governmental and private insurers for their services directly. They have been included in governmental payment programs, such as Medicaid, for decades. Historically, nurse midwives were paid only 65 percent of the comparable physician fee, but under the 2010 Patient Protection and Affordable Care Act (ACA), the payment level was increased to 100 percent of the physician fee for the same services. Nurse Midwives are included for reimbursement under private payment coverage plans as well. In the U.S., CNMs accept primarily low-risk patients for prenatal, birthing, and post-natal services. They may work with high-risk patients, but this is done under the supervision of an obstetrician/gynecologist. CNMs are also trained to provide care for other gynecological needs, such as meno-pausal problems and birth control.

- ■ **Certified Registered Nurse Anesthetists**
  - Certified registered nurse anesthetists (CRNAs) work in hospital and ambulatory surgery sites performing anesthetic services for surgical and diagnostic procedures. Nurse anesthetists function professionally as licensed independent practitioners or, depending on state law in individual states, may require some degree of direct supervision from the physician or surgeon who is performing the procedure at the time. In 31 states, there is no requirement for physician supervision of CRNAs in ambulatory surgical facilities. On April 6, 2020, CMS issued an emergency rule that waived the requirement for physician supervision of CRNAs in order to improve efficiency during the COVID-19 pandemic.
  - CRNAs practice in all 50 states of the United States. In their training, nurse anesthetists complete a four-year baccalaureate degree in nursing or a science-related subject and must successfully complete the licensing examination to become an RN. Prior to entering a specialized graduate-level program in nursing anesthesia, the nurse is required to gain at least one year of clinical experience as an RN in an acute care setting, such as a medical intensive care unit or surgical intensive care unit. Some programs require two or more years of clinical experience. Having gained the necessary experience, nurse applicants are eligible to enroll in an accredited program of anesthesia education for an additional two to three years during which they will receive a combination of intensive didactic education in nursing science, principles and theories, and clinical practice. Finally, in order to gain the designation of CRNA, the nurse must pass a mandatory national certification examination.
  - CRNAs remain the highest compensated of all nursing specialties. Their median reported annual salary as of May 2020, as reported by the Bureau of Labor Statistics, was $189,190. (8)

6.2.3 Licensed Practical Nurses

Licensed practical nurses (LPNs) or licensed vocational nurses (LVNs) work generally in physician practices, or at the bedside in hospitals, long-term care and home care. An LPN, called a licensed vocational nurse or LVN in some states, will have completed a 12- to 14-month post–high school educational program that focuses on basic nursing care. In the current environment of high demand for nursing personnel, some high schools are designing curricula that prepare the student to successfully complete a brief period of study prior to graduation or even to directly complete the licensing examination upon graduation from high school. In order to become an LPN, the individual must pass the NCLEX-PN licensing examination. In 2020, there were over 920,000 LPNs in the United States with a median annual pay of $48,820 according to the BLS. (9)

6.2.4 Nursing Supply

The United States faces an ongoing, serious nursing shortage as demographic pressures impact both the supply and demand for nurses.

The demand for RNs is expected to increase significantly particularly as baby boomers enter their retirement years and as healthcare coverage expands to increase access to care and in the face of the potential for future pandemics. As demographic shifts occur in the aging of the population and more people gain healthcare financial coverage, access to care may be limited unless the number of nurses and of other primary caregivers increases in proportion to the increase in demand.

From a supply perspective, there were approximately 3.8 million registered nurses (RNs) working in the United States in 2020, however some left the profession following the intense work experience of COVID-19 and others are nearing retirement. "With more than 500,000 seasoned RNs anticipated to retire by 2022, the U.S. Bureau of Labor Statistics projects the need for 1.1 million new RNs for expansion and replacement of retirees, and to avoid a nursing shortage." (10) According to a report published in 2018 in the *American Journal of Medical Quality*, "there will be a shortage of . . . 510,394 RNs by 2030; the South and West regions will have higher shortage ratios" than other parts of the country. (11)

While there is ongoing interest and investment in expanding the number and capacities of nursing schools throughout the United States to address growing demand, this may be only a partial solution to the problem of the ongoing nursing shortage. Studies of the drivers of the nursing shortage reveal that there are other systemic reasons that also need to be addressed in finding a permanent solution to this particular workforce issue. These drivers include the following:

■ Economic issues among nurses who feel there is not sufficient parity of their compensation with others working in clinical services

- New and expanding opportunities that are being made available for nurses to work in careers in which they are not providing direct patient care (e.g., in research institutions, sales functions, quality improvement organizations, information technology companies, payer organizations, and public policy bodies)
- The often stressful clinical work environment
- Insufficient staffing in inpatient units
- The pace and scheduling of work life and sometimes unpredictable shift schedules
- In 2020, nurses faced new challenges of increased burnout, the dangers of exposure to COVID-19 and emotional distress at seeing high numbers of patients die during the pandemic.

Each of these factors needs to be addressed in order to effectively respond to and resolve the serious shortage of nurses in the United States. With that shortage, there is danger of a diminishing both the quality of care in hospitals and other patient environments and of a negative effect on patient satisfaction.

6.3 Physician Assistants

Physician assistants (PAs) practice medicine with a substantial level of independence but under the supervision of physicians and surgeons. The more than 113,000 PAs in the United States have been formally trained to provide diagnostic, therapeutic, and preventive healthcare services. (12) Working as members of the healthcare team, they take patient medical histories, examine and treat patients, order and review laboratory tests and X-rays, make diagnoses, and prescribe medications. They also treat minor injuries by suturing, splinting, and casting.

While PAs work primarily under the supervision of a licensed physician, in some poor-access areas such as remote rural regions or clinics, PAs may be the only medical provider in the area. In these situations, they work under the direct, minimal supervision of a physician who spends only brief periods in the office or clinic in which the PA works. In all cases, the PA consults with the licensed physician as needed in complex cases that call on diagnostic and treatment skills beyond those for which the PA is licensed.

PAs are trained in the medical school model of education that includes both didactic learning in the classroom and application in the clinical or hospital setting. Most PA educational programs require the student to complete at least two years of undergraduate education with the inclusion of pre-medicine courses such as biology and chemistry in the curriculum. They then go on to PA training programs that typically last for 30 to 36 months. In total, they have at least four years of college education. In 2019, there were 240 accredited education programs in the U.S. for PAs according to the American Academy of Physician Assistants. (13) Before going into practice, all PAs are required to pass the Physician Assistant National Certifying Examination in order to be licensed by their state or the District of Columbia.

6.4 Pharmacists

There are over 310,000 pharmacists in the United States and their number is growing. (14) However, according to the BLS, there is an expected 2-percent decline in jobs between 2020 and 2030. (15) The majority of U.S. pharmacists work in retail pharmacies, most of which are owned by major corporate chains throughout the country. The remainder of pharmacists work in hospitals, research, government organizations, with payer plans, or in other related pharmaceutical fields.

In the hospital, the pharmacist supports the medication needs of both inpatients and outpatients. With the publication of the Institute of Medicine (IOM) report, *To Err is Human: Building a Safer Health System (published in 2000)* and *Crossing the Quality Chasm: A New Health System for the 21st Century (published 2001),* the role of pharmacists expanded significantly. In *To Err is Human*, the (IOM) reported that 98,000 deaths that occur in U.S. hospitals each year are due to preventable errors. A substantial portion of these are medication errors. Subsequent to the publication of the report, the work of pharmacists became focused not only on dispensing medications but also on the process of medication management and error reduction. This has required pharmacist involvement and leadership in the development and implementation of information systems for computerized provider order entry, for bar coding of medications, for medication management systems, and for the training and workflow change of everyone in the process chain of medication administration, from the physician to the nurse to the pharmacist.

The pharmacist's role, both in retail pharmacies and in hospitals, has been transformed in response to the increased demand for patient education and patient counseling in order to ensure that patients understand their medications and take them appropriately. This has become a core part of the role of pharmacists. They can expect their role to continue to evolve as the population ages and as the availability of new pharmaceuticals offers more and more opportunities for physicians and their patients to address medical problems through noninvasive interventions.

In hospitals the pharmacist's role encompasses a number of highly specialized areas, including nuclear pharmacy, intravenous therapy and services in adult medicine, pediatrics, ambulatory care oncology, psychiatry and other services offered by the hospital. The nature and size of the hospital help determine the extent to which these specialized services are needed. Because of the diversity of activities involved in hospital pharmacy departments, the pharmacist manager is expected to provide management expertise, including finance and budgeting, personnel administration, systems development, and planning.

Pharmacy education varies slightly from school to school. All schools of pharmacy offer the Doctor of Pharmacy (PharmD) degree, which requires six years of education. In pursuing this education, the student is provided both the didactic experience of the classroom and the interactive experience of working in practice internships. Upon completion of their PharmD, the aspiring pharmacist must complete a licensing examination called the North American Pharmacist Licensure Examination™ (NAPLEX®), which is administered by the National Association of Boards of Pharmacy.

6.5 Medical Technologists

Medical technologists (MT) or Clinical Laboratory Technologists (CLTs) work in the laboratory and are responsible for the wide variety of laboratory tests on bodily fluids and tissues that are ordered for diagnostic purposes. The medical technologist works under the supervision of a director (or other related position) of laboratory services and under the oversight of a pathologist. The medical technologist completes four years of college-level training in clinical laboratory science, which includes several years of classroom study and at least one year of clinical internship rotations. In practice, he or she is supported by medical laboratory technicians (MLTs) or clinical laboratory technicians (CLAs) who are prepared through a two-year associate degree. Eleven states and Puerto Rico require the medical technologist to complete a licensing examination and maintain that license in order to practice. Other states seek documentation that the technologist is certified by the American Society of Clinical Pathologists (ASCP). With this certification, they carry the related professional designation after their names.

6.6 Radiology Technologists

Radiology technologists (RTs) staff the X-ray services at hospitals, health systems, ambulatory centers, diagnostic radiology centers, and other related sites. According to the Bureau of Labor Statistics, the field of radiology technology is expected to grow faster than average among occupations in the U.S. Employment of radiology technologists is expected to increase by 7 percent from 2019 to 2029. (16)

The role of radiology technologists is primarily to perform diagnostic imaging examinations on patients. This requires preparing the equipment and patients for radiology exams, completing the imaging, and then sending the images to radiologists and physicians who ordered the tests. Each radiology image is reviewed by a radiologist who writes the interpretive clinical report of findings. The images are also frequently used directly by the ordering physician for diagnosis.

Radiology technologists are prepared for their profession typically through four years of college education that is composed of several years in the classroom and rotation or internship in a radiology department. Certification by the American Registry of Radiologic Technologists and/or a license to practice is required by most states and by employers. With increased technologic and diagnostic innovations (such as MRI) and expanded clinical use of radiologic procedures and equipment, for example in the treatment of cancer, radiology technologists have the opportunity to specialize in their field.

RTs are supported by radiology technicians, whose training at the associate degree level or below prepare them to perform basic X-ray procedures and to prepare films and equipment for the technologist, as well as to perform other supportive functions in the department such as helping patients to the examination room and preparing them for the procedure.

Currently, there are over 700 training programs available to students interested in a career in radiology technology. Professionals in this field tend to earn slightly less than their counterparts in other clinical areas.

6.7 Physical, Occupational, and Speech Therapists

Physical, occupational, and speech therapists work in the hospitals that offer rehabilitation units as well as in private practice and in independent, free-standing rehabilitation centers. Each of these professionals focuses on a different area of recuperative therapy.

6.7.1 Physical Therapists

Physical therapists provide services that help restore function, improve mobility, relieve pain, and prevent or limit permanent physical disabilities of patients suffering from injuries or disease. They restore, maintain, and promote overall fitness and health. Their patients include accident victims, post-surgical patients, and individuals with disabling conditions such as low-back pain, arthritis, heart disease, fractures, head injuries, and cerebral palsy.

Educationally, physical therapists complete a doctorate in physical therapy (DPT) following their bachelor's degree program. The DPT program requires both classroom didactic study and experiential application in a clinical setting. Upon receiving a DPT from a program accredited by CAPTE (Commission on Accreditation of Physical Therapy Education), and prior to entering into practice, the physical therapist graduate must successfully complete the National Physical Therapy Exam (NPTE) which is provided by the Federation of State Boards of Physical Therapy (FSBPT). Upon successful completion of the exam, the PT must acquire a license in order to practice in his or her state of choice. Following licensure, the PT may continue their education through a residency or fellowship program in order to become board-certified in a PT specialty.

6.7.2 Speech and Language Pathologists

The title of speech therapist is self-explanatory of the work of the professional. Also known as speech-language pathologists, speech therapists work with people who have any of an array of speech disorders. They work in hospitals as well as in schools and other settings in which a speech or language disorder may be diagnosed early and corrected. A language disorder is one in which the individual has difficulty understanding what others are saying or to express himself or herself or have a speech disorder related to a difficulty in making sounds that are correct and fluent.

Each professional in this field requires a master's degree, must pass the Praxis Examination in Speech-Language Pathology which is commissioned and adopted by the American Speech-Language-Hearing Association (ASHA) and must be licensed in their respective state in order to practice.

6.7.3 Occupational Therapists

The registered occupational therapist (OTR) focuses on education and functional training of the patient and their participation in daily activities. The OTR works with the patient to help him or her regain the ability to perform activities of daily living (ADLs), such as cooking, driving, bathing, working with the computer, and so on.

Occupational therapists complete a masters and/or doctoral degree from an educational program that is accredited by the Accreditation Council for Occupational Therapy Education (ACOTE). OTRs are required to successfully complete the national examination for certification of the National Board for Certification in Occupational Therapy (NBCOT) before entering practice. In all states in the United States, they are required to be licensed.

6.8 Other Allied Health Professionals and Researchers

While nursing, by its sheer numbers, is the largest single clinical profession in the hospital or health system, many other licensed and certified professionals comprise the aggregate field of "allied health professionals." Throughout the hospital and other healthcare delivery settings, there are a number of licensed personnel who do not necessarily work at the bedside, and so are less visible to the patients, but are nonetheless essential to the services that are performed for the patient. They include registered dietitians, social workers, psychologists, recreation therapists, and others

Researchers have a key role to play in healthcare. They function in academic medical centers and in teaching hospitals, pharmaceutical and other companies, education, public health, government agencies and in other venues. They work at the forefront of medical science finding and developing new drugs, clinical procedures, medical and supportive equipment, insight into diseases and medical and information technologies that advance medical care. Within the community of researchers are physicians, nurses, and other scientists. Researchers in medical science are often required to perform human clinical trials to test new drugs and technologies. When this is the case, they are required to obtain the approval of an Institutional Review Board (IRB). An IRB exists in all U.S. research institutions to ensure that research of any kind involving humans is done within defined ethical standards

6.9 Supporting Professionals

Hospitals and health systems cannot function without other nonclinical professionals, many of whom are licensed in their fields and work behind the scenes of patient care. These include the engineers whose attention is on the buildings and facilities; environmental specialists whose focus is on the cleanliness and orderliness of the facilities; safety managers who address hazards for employees, patients, and others; financial professionals whose role is in accounting, billing, payroll, and other financial functions; supply managers who ensure that clinical, food, environmental, and other supplies are on hand and available as needed; and administrative professionals in management, marketing, human resources, information technology, community relations, planning, facility development, fundraising, and other key roles. Additionally, other supporting professionals work directly with patients in roles such as care coordinators, and chaplains. Many of these roles exist not only in hospitals but also in nursing care facilities, specialty services, large physician practices, and networks of providers of care.

6.10 Administrative Management Professionals

Finally, a discussion of the professionals in the healthcare provider workforce would not be complete without the inclusion of those whose responsibility it is to set the direction for the healthcare enterprise and manage and direct it organizationally so that all the elements work together coherently and efficiently. The field of healthcare management is responsible for providing leadership, strategic vision, structure, and direction to organizations that are very complex. The C-suite executives and mid-level management team provide administrative direction and leadership to the organization, with the support of administrative personnel. The C-suite includes the following:

- Chief Executive Officer (CEO); President and CEO
- Chief Operating Officer (COO)
- Chief Financial Officer (CFO)

- Chief Information Officer (CIO)
- Chief Medical Officer (CMO)
- Chief Nursing Officer (CNO)
- Vice Presidents
- Executive Vice Presidents
- Others

They are also responsible for directing and managing the organization's relationship with the external environment. That environment imposes extensive federal, state, and local rules and regulations on the organization, a public and patients who are demanding, payer organizations with whom the administrators must negotiate reimbursement rates and financing mechanisms, vendors of the thousands of products used in the healthcare system each day, governance structures, community organizations and members, competitors, and other economic and environmental forces that impact the business of the organization.

Administrators in healthcare provider organizations are generally educationally prepared in master's programs in health administration or business administration. These programs are situated in a variety of academic settings, including schools of medicine, of public health, business administration and allied health sciences. Many in administrative and leadership roles are clinical professionals such as doctors and nurses who have prepared themselves for organizational management. Persons entering the field of health administration at an entry level may be prepared in a bachelor's degree program; however, an advanced degree is typically required in order for them to enter the ranks of upper management. In addition to the MHA (Masters of Health Administration), degrees such as the MPH (Masters of Public Health), MHSA (Masters of Health Services Administration), and MBA (Masters of Business Administration) are valued among the senior management ranks.

6.11 Nursing Facility Administration

The requirement for practice as a nursing home administrator is quite different from that of the hospital administrator. Nursing home administrators may come from any of a number of educational programs and may have clinical or management experience. While they do not have a defined educational requirement in most states, nursing home administrators are required to pass

a licensing examination in order to be licensed as a nursing home administrator in the state in which the facility is located. This examination is typically administered by the National Association of Boards of Examiners of
Long-Term Care Administrators. Some states require a bachelor's degree or
other formal education to qualify for the licensing exam.

6.12 Summary

Healthcare is composed of a wide array of clinicians and nonclinical professionals. Their training is extensive, and the opportunity for career growth is
expansive. Their professions require that they complete rigorous education
programs and successfully complete a licensure examination in the state in
which they practice. While the United States continues to expand its educational opportunities for the various clinical professions, the country faces a
near-term shortage of many nurses and other clinicians. A solution to that
shortage is one that will require creativity, funding, and expansion of training programs if it is to be addressed effectively. The historical approach
of recruiting from other countries only to leave them bereft of the workforce to meet their own needs is increasingly frowned upon in the global
community.

References

1. American Nurses Association. *Workforce.* Available at www.nursingworld.org/
   practice-policy/workforce/.
2. M.B. Schnur. 2020 (May 28). U.S. nurses in 2020: Who we are and where
   we work. *Nursing Center Blog.* Available at www.nursingcenter.com/ncblog/
   may-2020/u-s-nurses-in-2020.
3. American Association of Colleges of Nursing. 2021 (Apr. 1). *Student enrollment surged in U.S. schools of nursing in 2020 despite challenges presented
   by the pandemic.* Available at www.aacnnursing.org/News-Information/
   Press-Releases/View/ArticleId/24802/2020-survey-data-student-enrollment.
4. American Association of Colleges of Nursing. 2019 (Apr.). *Fact sheet: The
   impact of education on nursing practice.* Available at www.aacnnursing.org/
   Portals/42/News/Factsheets/Education-Impact-Fact-Sheet.pdf.
5. American Association of Colleges of Nursing. 2020. *Employment of new
   nurse graduates and employer preferences for baccalaureate-prepared nurses.*
   Available at www.aacnnursing.org/News-Information/Research-Data-Center/
   Employment/2020.

6. U.S. Bureau of Labor Statistics. Last modified date, 2021 (Apr. 9). *Occupational Outlook handbook: Nurse anesthetists, nurse midwives, and nurse practitioners.* www.bls.gov/ooh/healthcare/nurse-anesthetists-nurse-midwives-and-nurse-practitioners.htm.

7. D. Fang and K. Kesten. 2017 (Sept.–Oct.). Retirements and success of nursing faculty in 2016–2025. *Nursing Outlook*, 65(5): 633–642. doi: 10.1016/j.outlook.2017.03.003. Available at https://pubmed.ncbi.nlm.nih.gov/28579147/.

8. Bureau of Labor Statistics. 2020 (May). Occupational employment and wages. *29–1151 Nurse Anesthetists.* Available at www.bls.gov/oes/current/oes291151.htm. And at www.bls.gov/ooh/healthcare/nurse-anesthetists-nurse-midwives-and-nurse-practitioners.htm.

9. Bureau of Labor Statistics. 2021. *Occupational outlook handbook: Licensed practical nurses and licensed vocational nurses.* Available at www.bls.gov/ooh/healthcare/licensed-practical-and-licensed-vocational-nurses.htm.

10. Bureau of Labor Statistics. 2021. Occupational outlook handbook. *Registered Nurses.* Available at www.bls.gov/ooh/healthcare/registered-nurses.html.

11. X. Zhang, D. Tai, H. Pforsich and V.W. Lin. 2018 (May/June). United States registered nurse workforce report card and shortage forecast: A revisit. *American Journal of Medical Quality*, 33(3): 229–236.

12. Kaiser Family Foundation. *Total number of physician assistants, by gender.* Available at www.kff.org/other/state-indicator/total-physician-assistants/?currentTimeframe=0&sortModel=%7B%22colId%22:%22Location%22,%22sort%22:%22asc%22%7D.

13. A. Durani. 2019 (June 11). Consider a physician assistant program as an international student. *U. S. News.* Available at www.usnews.com/education/best-graduate-schools/articles/2019-06-11/consider-a-physician-assistant-program-as-an-international-student#:~:text=There%20are%20currently%20more%20than%20240%20accredited%20physician,which%20represents%20PA%20educational%20programs%20in%20the%20U.S.

14. M. Mikulic. 2020 (Sept. 20). Number of pharmacists in the U.S. 2001–2019. *Statista.* Available at www.statista.com/statistics/185723/number-of-pharmacists-in-the-us-since-2001/.

15. Bureau of Labor Statistics. *Occupational Outlook handbook: Pharmacists.* Available at www.bls.gov/ooh/healthcare/pharmacists.htm. Last modified April 9, 2021.

16. Bureau of Labor Statistics. *Occupational Outlook handbook: Radiologic and MRI technologists.* Available at www.bls.gov/ooh/healthcare/radiologic-technologists.htm.

Chapter 7

Chapter 7

The Legal and Regulatory Environment

7.1 Introduction

The government's role in healthcare delivery is threefold. The government serves as a *payer* of healthcare, as a *provider* of healthcare, and as a *regulator* of healthcare. Each of these roles is distinct, and each has its own impact on the delivery of healthcare.

At the federal level, the government serves as a payer of healthcare through programs such as Medicare, Medicaid, the Veterans Administration, the Indian Health Services, the ACA, and other such structures. State governments are also payers of healthcare through their administration and funding of Medicaid, the State Children's Health Insurance Program, mental health services, and public health services. Likewise, local governments participate in both paying for and providing healthcare services through their financial support and/or ownership of screening, diagnostic, and treatment clinics and hospitals owned and operated by a county or city.

As providers of healthcare, federal, state, and local governments own and operate direct service care facilities. For example, the federal government owns and operates the Veterans Administration hospitals and the Indian Health Services hospitals and clinics. Many states own and operate mental health facilities and prison hospitals, and at the local level some counties and local city governments own and operate hospitals (e.g., Grady Health System in Atlanta owned by the Fulton-DeKalb Hospital Authority, John H. Stroger, Jr. Hospital of Cook County in Chicago).

DOI: 10.4324/9781003202950-7

The role of government as regulator is the one we tend to recognize first when we think of the government in healthcare. A plethora of laws and regulations control and direct the ways and methods by which healthcare is delivered from the most fundamental issues of sanitation to the more complex areas of financing, medical sciences (e.g., research and drug approvals) and technology.

In this chapter, we address primarily the role of government as regulator. Its role as payer will come into the discussion in Chapter 8 on financing of healthcare. Its role as provider was discussed in Chapter 3 on the structures of healthcare delivery services.

7.1.1 The Government as Regulator

The government regulates healthcare in a wide variety of areas from the most basic realms of cleanliness for infection control to the licensing of clinical professionals, to the more complex realms of capital financing and approvals of new drugs, and many other functions. As regulator, the impact of governmental requirements comes not only from the legislative branch but also from the executive and judicial branches. The legislative branch passes laws, the executive branch implements those laws through detailed regulations that guide their execution, and the judicial branch issues decisions that interpret the law when there is disagreement about its meaning or intent.

Within the executive branch of the government, the Department of Health and Human Services (DHHS) holds primary responsibility for the implementation of statutes regulating healthcare. Public health agencies which are part of DHHS have responsibility to protect and advance the health of the population. They are discussed in Chapter 11, "Public Health" where a description of the various major public health departments and agencies of the federal government are presented.

7.2 The Legislature: Healthcare Statutes

While a plethora of laws have converged upon healthcare providers over the past centuries, this discussion will focus on a number of the laws of the past several decades that have a major and widespread impact on healthcare. A comprehensive review of major healthcare legislation can be easily accessed through one of the major Internet search engines. Table 7.1 provides a partial list of major legislative initiatives affecting healthcare in the United States since 1946.

Table 7.1 Chronology of Major Healthcare Legislation in the U.S.

1946	Hospital Survey and Construction Act (Hill–Burton Act), PL 79-725
1949	Hospital Construction Act, PL 81-380
1950	Public Health Services Act Amendments, PL 81-692
1955	Poliomyelitis Vaccination Assistance Act, PL 84-377
1956	Health Research Facilities Act, PL 84-835
1960	Social Security Amendments (Kerr-Mill Aid), PL 86-778
1961	Community Health Services and Facilities Act, PL 87-395
1962	Public Health Service Act, PL 87-838
	Vaccination Assistance, PL 87-868
1963	Mental Retardation Facilities Construction Act/Community Mental Health Centers Act, PL 88-164
1964	Nurse Training Act, PL 88-581
1965	Community Health Services and Facilities Act, PL 89-109
	Medicare and Medicaid, PL 89-97
	Mental Health Centers Act Amendments, PL 89-105
	Heart Disease, Cancer, and Stroke Amendments, PL 89-239
1966	Comprehensive Health Planning and Service Act, PL 89-749
1970	Community Mental Health Service Act, PL 91-211
	Family Planning Services and Population Research Act, PL 91-572
	Lead-Based Paint Poisoning Prevention Act, PL 91-695
1971	National Cancer Act, PL 92-218
1973	Health Maintenance Organization Act, PL 93-222
1974	Research on Aging Act, PL 93-296
	National Health Planning and Resources Development Act (Created CON), PL 93-641
1979	Department of Education Organization Act (Created HHS), PL 96-88
1982	Tax Equity and Fiscal Responsibility Act (TEFRA), PL 97-248
1983	Amendments to the Social Security Act (Prospective Payment System), PL 106-113
1985	Consolidated Omnibus Reconciliation Act (COBRA), PL 99-272

(Continued)

Table 7.1 (*Continued*)

1987	Department of Transportation Appropriations Act, PL 100-202
	Omnibus Budget Reconciliation Act (OBRA), PL 100-203
1988	Medicare Catastrophic Coverage Act, PL 100-360
1989	Department of Transportation and Related Agencies Appropriations Act, PL 101-164
1993	Family and Medical Leave Act, PL 103-3
1996	Health Insurance Portability and Accountability Act, PL 104-191
1997	Balanced Budget Act (BBA), PL 105-33
2002	Public Health Security and Bioterrorism Preparedness and Response Act, PL 107-188
2005	Patient Safety and Quality Improvement Act, PL 109-41
2008	Mental Health Parity and Addiction Equity Act, H.R. 4058
2009	American Reinvestment and Recovery Act (ARRA) which includes the HITECH Act to support implementation of the EHR PL 111-5
2010	Patient Protection and Affordable Care Act (PPACA), PL 111-48

7.2.1 Hill–Burton

During World War II and in its immediate aftermath, large employers were providing healthcare insurance for their employees. With improved and expanded financial access to medical care, the demand for healthcare services increased dramatically. However, access to hospitals was limited because there were not enough inpatient beds in which to meet the growing demand. With a report on hand from the Commission on Hospital Care indicating a need for 195,000 beds across the country, particularly in poorer and rural areas, U.S. Senators Lister Hill (D-AL) and Harold Burton (R-OH) sponsored the Hospital Survey and Construction Act in 1946, which came to be known as the Hill–Burton Act. The legislation was intended to fund the development of new and replacement hospitals and nursing homes in underserved areas. Its initial 5-year commitment of $75 million in funding through grants and loans was extended into subsequent years. By 1968, it had provided funding for 9,200 hospitals and other medical facilities, expanding bed capacity by 416,000 new beds. (1) The Hill–Burton Act was still funding hospital construction until 1997. Next to the enactment of the Medicare and Medicaid legislation in the 1960s, the Hill–Burton program was one of the most impactful federal initiatives to advance and transform healthcare in the U.S.–it drove the building of the infrastructure needed to make healthcare widely available throughout the country.

The hospital building boom that was generated by the Hill–Burton program carried a proviso for each of the hospitals that received funding. That proviso required the hospital to provide assurance that it would be available to the community in perpetuity and that it would provide free or subsidized charity care to people who were unable to pay. However, the level of charity care was not defined, nor was there a time limit on how long the requirement to provide charity care would continue. It was not until court decisions and regulatory actions were taken in the 1960s and 1970s that the time commitment for the provision of charity care was established as a 20-year time frame from initial Hill–Burton funding of a building/expansion project.

Under the Hill–Burton program, hospital capacity in the United States expanded dramatically. Many small communities came to have "their own" hospital, and they took pride in the presence of a hospital in their communities. Doctors were attracted to small communities knowing they would have a hospital in which to care for their acute care patients, perform surgical procedures, birth babies, and generally provide a level of acute care for their patients that they could not do in their offices. While this sense of security and expansion prevailed, many uninsured indigent and elderly people did not have adequate access to care.

After 20+ years of building hospitals throughout the country, a heightened awareness developed of the new problem: there were large numbers of people who could not access those hospitals because they did not have the wherewithal to pay for services and the hospitals could not financially support the volume of free care that would be needed. In rural communities, the poor and the elderly who comprised a large proportion of the population were being left behind while hospitals were concerned about their financial viability in the face of their indigent care commitment. They were obliged to care for the indigent under their Hill–Burton funding, but they had not planned for the volume impact of charity care on their operational finances.

7.2.2 Medicare and Medicaid (Titles XVIII and XIX of the Social Security Amendments)

Awareness of the cost of charity care across the country led directly to the introduction of Medicare and Medicaid in 1965. Legislation enacting the two programs was signed by President Lyndon Johnson on July 30, 1965. The two programs have a similar goal to make healthcare accessible for the poor and elderly respectively, but beyond that they are very distinct from one another.

Medicare Part A (hospital insurance) was designed to pay for hospital care, home healthcare and limited skilled nursing care for persons age 65 and over regardless of their income level. Medicare Part B (medical insurance) was designed to cover physician services and to be optional to the enrollee. By 1972, the Social Security amendments that established Medicare were expanded to include coverage for persons of all ages with end-stage renal disease (ESRD) and with long-term disabilities who would qualify for Medicare.

Medicare is administered and funded by the Centers for Medicare and Medicaid Services (CMS). CMS contracts with, and works through, regional designated fiscal intermediaries, such as Blue Cross/Blue Shield companies, in the administration of the program.

Medicaid was designed to provide insurance coverage of medical and long-term care for the poor and disabled. It is administered by the States and funded in part by the federal government through CMS. Until the PPACA persons who were eligible for Medicaid included those unable to work and whose incomes were under the designated federal poverty level. Generally, if a person received less than 100 percent to 200 percent of the federal poverty level and was either pregnant, elderly, disabled, a parent/caretaker, or child, that person was a likely candidate for Medicaid healthcare coverage. The PPACA expanded the eligible population by including parents and adults without children. In other words, all persons under age 65 with incomes below 133 percent of the federal poverty level became eligible in those states that adopted the program expansion provided in the PPACA. As of August 2021, 38 states had chosen to do so. In 2021, the Federal poverty level was set at an annual income of $12,880 for a single person, and at $26,500 for a family of four in the contiguous 48 states. (2)

For Medicare enrollees who are within the poverty level, Medicaid serves as supplemental or "gap" insurance which provides coverage for costs that Medicare does not cover such as deductibles and co-insurance.

While the passage of Medicare and Medicaid in 1965 was a watershed day for healthcare in the United States, cost began to rise beyond budgeted forecasts. In the decades since the implementation of these programs, healthcare costs have continued to escalate, generally beyond the consumer price index, the CPI. By 2019, according to CMS, Medicare spending was approximately $800.7 billion and was expected to grow at an annual rate of 7.6 percent from 2019–2028. (3)

7.2.3 Certificate of Need

Until the early 1970s, Congress and the administration had tried a number of cost containment methods to control the upward spiraling costs of Medicare and Medicaid, most were to little avail in accomplishing a reversal of the dramatic cost increase trend that persisted following the implementation of Medicare and Medicaid. By the early 1970s, the legislature determined that the building boom introduced by the Hill–Burton program had to be controlled. It was decided by policy makers that healthcare dollars spent on construction and equipment needed to be spent based on a planned determination of population need for health services (i.e., the need for acute care beds, nursing homes, etc.).

What ensued was passage of the Health Planning and Resources Development Act, Section 93-641 of the Social Security Act in 1974, better known as the Certificate of Need law (CON). The intent of the legislators was twofold: (1) to ensure that health facility and service expenditures being made in the private and public sectors were for services needed by the community or region and (2) to reduce the duplication of expensive facilities and services that was occurring in many areas.

The statute provided for formalized community planning of the needed healthcare services and called upon each state to enact and implement laws for (1) the establishment of planning agencies to lead the development of statewide health plans that would identify needed (or excess) healthcare resources and (2) the creation of a certificate of need program to review and approve or disapprove major capital expenditures for expansion of capacity or creation of new services by healthcare providers.

While CON became the best-known part of the Health Planning and Resources Development Act, the first part of the law called on each state to create and adopt a plan for health services based on population need. Under Section 93-641, states were required to create a health planning function in which analysis of population and an inventory of existing facilities and services could be developed by local communities and used to craft a state-wide health plan. Based primarily on this, community needs would be assessed and used to determine the level of services and number of hospitals and long-term care beds needed to adequately serve the population.

CON decisions for healthcare expansion and facility replacement would be made by the State based on an assessment of each project against the state health plan. The requirement for CON approval of capital expenditure projects was designed to slow the duplication of healthcare facilities and services. The new CON laws placed both civil and criminal penalties on providers of care who undertook major capital expenditures or who expanded into new services without the requisite CON approval. The intent of this law was to ultimately reduce the rate of cost increase in healthcare.

Much controversy swirled around many capital projects as they moved forward in the local and state public review process. That process was open to statements and documentation from other providers in the geographic area of the applicant organization, to consumers, to employers, and to anyone from the public who wanted to have input. Thus, competitive forces were introduced into the process. Competitors, neighbors, and consumers could be vocal in support of or disagreement with a project application.

Overall, the intended impact of CON to reduce the rate of increase in the costs of healthcare in the United States was not realized. In the face of a continuing high pace of healthcare cost increases, the federal government sunset (i.e., repealed) the statute in 1987, and states were authorized to repeal their respective CON laws. Some states repealed their CON requirements, but 35 states and the District of Columbia continue to use state level health planning agencies to maintain a CON review of healthcare capital expenditures in their states. These review programs serve as a barrier to entry and to expansion in so far as existing hospitals and other providers of care are sustained in their markets and competitors can be denied entry. They also serve to constrain overbuilding and expensive duplication of services.

7.2.4 The Health Maintenance Organization Act

The Health Maintenance Organization Act or HMO Act of 1973 is important in that it supported the widespread development of HMOs. Up until that time, HMOs were in place in various areas throughout the country; however, they were not flourishing. Because HMOs focused on primary and preventive care, on case management, and on controlling costs, the HMO Act of 1973 was intended to be part of a cost-containment initiative. Its goal was to reduce healthcare costs by eliminating regulatory barriers that inhibited HMO development. Under the HMO Act of 1973, HMOs could be designated for federal qualification by meeting certain mandates related to their benefits packages, open enrollment, and community rating. With federal certification, they could go to employers who had 25 or more employees to present their plan to employees, and those employers were then required to offer the HMO option to their employees. While this latter provision was eliminated in 1995, during the early years of its existence HMOs were boosted onto the U.S. healthcare "stage" under the 1973 mandate. That widespread visibility of the HMO and its focus on primary care and case/cost management helped to prepare the U.S. healthcare system, insurers, employers, and the public for managed care in the early to mid-1990s. (4) Today HMO-like structures are included in Medicare under what are now "Medicare Advantage" plans.

Medicare Advantage Plans provide Medicare Part A and Part B coverage, and in many cases, they provide coverage of drugs under Part D. These plans are offered by Medicare-approved private companies and require enrollees to use healthcare providers who are in their networks or pay high costs if they go out of network. A limit is set on the enrollee's annual out-of-pocket cost helping to protect the enrolled person or family from unexpected charges as long as they stay in network. The most common types of Medicare Advantage Plans are:

- Health Maintenance Organization (HMO) Plans. In these plans, enrollees must access services from a provider in the plan's network, with few exceptions such as emergency care. Costs are generally lower to the enrollee and many plans include coverage of drug costs. If an enrollee uses an out-of-network provider, that enrollee may have to pay the full costs of care charged by that provider. Referrals to specialists are required as is pre-approval for certain services.
- Preferred Provider Organization (PPO) Plans. PPOs in Medicare Advantage Plans offer a network of doctors, hospitals, and other providers, but costs will be higher when an out-of-network provider is used. These plans may offer more benefits than Original Medicare but at higher costs.
- Private Fee-for-Service (PPF) Plans. These private plans determine how much they'll pay for doctor, hospital and other provider services in a given area and providers in the area may or may not decide to accept Medicare Advantage PPF patients.
- Special Needs Plans (SNPs). SNPs limit enrollment to persons with specific diseases or characteristics.

(4)

7.2.5 *Prospective Payment*

Neither CON nor the HMO Act served effectively to sustainably reduce the rate of increase in healthcare costs. Costs continued to rise beyond the rate of the consumer price index. In yet another effort to control healthcare costs, Congress passed the Tax Equity and Fiscal Responsibility Act of 1982 (also known as TEFRA) which called for a case-based payment system for hospital inpatient care. Under this law, a prospective payment system was established for hospitals in which a predetermined fee was established (i.e., "prospective" fee) based on the diagnosis for which the patient was admitted.

TEFRA was implemented in 1983 and was significant in that it transitioned hospitals from the historic fee-for-service reimbursement approach to one based on diagnosis-related groups or DRGs. The structure of the payment system established "a patient classification scheme which provides a means of relating the type of patients a hospital treats to the costs incurred by the hospital" in caring for those patients. (5) In this structure, hospital reimbursement is based on predetermined rates. The diagnosis for which the patient is treated is the determining factor under which the provider is paid. If resources, such as days of care, over and above those that are predetermined to be needed to treat the diagnosis are used, the hospital does not get paid for the additional costs unless they can justify the longer stay, and vice versa, if the hospital can treat the patient at a lower use of resources, then the hospital still gets paid the established reimbursement rate.

This rate is determined based on the case mix of the hospital (i.e., the mix of patients that it serves and the acuity of their illness or injury) and on the average costs that should be required to provide needed service to address each patient's diagnosis. This structure reversed the practice of prior decades in which physicians and hospitals were generally unchallenged in their cost and pricing decision-making.

Initially, the DRG payment system applied only to hospitals and inpatient care. Ambulatory care, rehabilitation care, long-term care, and other venues were not impacted. One of the unintended consequences of the prospective payment system was to trigger a shift in care sites from the inpatient setting to these other venues. Patients who previously might have been admitted to the hospital were instead, whenever possible, referred to a non-acute care unit or provider (e.g., rehabilitation, sub-acute care, ambulatory surgical unit). Consequently, the decade following the implementation of DRGs was marked by substantial expansion of outpatient services–until, of course, DRG methods of reimbursement came to be applied to each of them in turn over the next decade. Within the Centers for Medicare and Medicaid Services (CMS), the Prospective Payment Advisory Commission is mandated to review regularly the payment system under which providers are reimbursed and to report to Congress on any changes that it advises.

The DRG system brought with it another potential unintended issue–that of providers who might forego diagnostic or treatment procedures for a patient in favor of saving monies that they would be paid under the preset fee. However, TEFRA provisions called for the establishment of physician review organizations that would be established to counter this "perverse incentive" through review of quality of care and ensure that quality did not suffer as a result of the payment system. In other words, quality improvement became part of the equation in the implementation of the prospective payment system.

7.2.6 *Emergency Medical Treatment and Active Labor Act*

The Emergency Medical Treatment and Active Labor Act (EMTALA) "is a statute which governs when and how a patient may be (1) refused treatment or (2) transferred from one hospital to another when they are in an unstable medical condition" (6) EMTALA affects almost every function of emergency departments today.

EMTALA was passed as part of the Consolidated Omnibus Budget Reconciliation Act of 1986 and is integrated into the Social Security Act under Section 1867(a). EMTALA evolved out of the policy that some hospitals employed to transfer uninsured patients from their emergency departments to public hospitals (In healthcare parlance, this is called "patient dumping."). Public hospitals are supported in part by local taxes and generally serve a much larger portion of the indigent population or those covered by Medicaid than do private hospitals. This practice placed a burden on public hospitals and placed the patient at risk in situations when they urgently needed medical attention. In some cases, patients were transferred when they were in the throes of the emergency condition for which they needed medical care, e.g., a pregnant woman in advanced labor.

"EMTALA is primarily but not exclusively a non-discrimination statute. One would cover most of its purpose and effect by characterizing it as providing that no patient who presents with an emergency medical condition and who is unable to pay may be treated differently than patients who are covered by health insurance. That is not the entire scope of EMTALA, however; it imposes affirmative obligations which go beyond non-discrimination." (6)

The core provisions of the law cover any patient who "comes to the emergency department" requesting "examination or treatment for a medical condition" and requires that the hospital provide "an appropriate medical screening examination." If it is determined that the patient has an emergency condition, then the hospital is obliged either to provide treatment until the patient is stabilized or transfer that patient to another hospital. That transfer may happen only under certain circumstances, such as the first hospital's lack of the specialty service that the patient needs. If it is determined that the patient can only receive the needed service at another facility that has the technology and specialty-trained personnel, then the hospital may be able to transfer the patient with the consent of the receiving hospital and with the provision of appropriately medically supported transport.

"A pregnant woman who presents in active labor must, for all practical purposes, be admitted and treated until delivery is completed, unless a transfer under the statute is appropriate." (6) "In essence, then, the statute imposes:

- an affirmative obligation on the part of the hospital to provide a medical screening examination to determine whether an 'emergency medical condition' exists;
- restrictions on transfers of persons who exhibit an 'emergency medical condition' or are in active labor, which restrictions may or may not be limited to transfers made for economic reasons; [and]
- an affirmative duty to institute treatment if an 'emergency medical condition' does exist."

(6)

7.2.7 Stark Law: The Physician Self-Referral Act (Stark I-1989 and Stark II-1993)

Named after Representative Pete Stark (D-CA), the Stark laws were passed as measures to prevent the abuse of referral arrangements by physicians to diagnostic services or other services in which they have an ownership interest. After research reports indicated that physicians were "reaping inordinate profits from Medicare because they were referring patients to their own facilities and ordering unnecessary tests," (7) Stark I was passed in 1989 to constrain the ability of physicians to refer patients for tests to facilities that they themselves own. In other words, physicians are prohibited from "referring Medicare patients to facilities with which they have a financial relationship." (7) Stark II was passed into law only four years later in order to further constrain the financial relationships between hospitals and doctors and to prevent doctors from referring to the inpatient and outpatient services of hospitals in which they own an interest unless they meet one of the list of exceptions provided in the law, also known as "safe harbors."

As healthcare evolved into the twenty-first century, the Stark laws came to be seen as a major hindrance to some of the positive initiatives that were needed to ensure quality of care and to reduce costs, primarily the adoption of the shared Electronic Health Record (EHR) among providers and the integration of medical care through the EHR. The key driver of concern was the illegality of hospitals investing in physician practices in order to support them in the cost of EHR implementation and interoperability for sharing patient information between the hospital and doctor.

Because the Stark laws were a major barrier to the adoption of the EHR, the rules and regulations implementing Stark were further modified in 2007 in order to allow hospitals to enter into limited financial arrangements with the doctors on their medical staff. Under the new provisions, hospitals can support EHR implementation in the offices of their doctors. These provisions require that software be integrated between the physician's office and the hospital and that there be networking and sharing of data between the physician practice and the hospital. This modification in Stark opened the way for hospitals and physicians to develop shared electronic systems for the storing, accessing, and sharing of patient data which is key to the integration of patient care across a continuum of care or wherever the patient seeks care in the health provider system.

7.2.8 HIPAA

"HIPAA" has been engrained into the consciousness of almost every healthcare worker in the United States. It has become a synonym for "privacy and security." Actually, HIPAA is an acronym for the Health Insurance Portability and Accountability Act of 1996, Public Law 104-191, which amended the Internal Revenue Service Code of 1986.

HIPAA was passed in an era of economic boom (just before the "dot com bust") when unemployment was low and many people found themselves in "job lock," unable to take advantage of better jobs because an existing medical condition would exclude them from their new employer's coverage for one year or more for that condition. Many employees with personal or family preexisting medical conditions could not afford to move up in their careers by moving to a position with a new employer because employers' health plans typically excluded coverage of persons with preexisting conditions for one year or more. The cost of healthcare served as a disincentive to employees who, while awaiting coverage with the new employer, would pay more in private payment for medical care and drugs than the increase in income they might enjoy in the new job–they were in job lock.

To break the hold of job lock, Congress passed the Kennedy–Kassebaum Act, now known simply as HIPAA. Under its Title I, HIPAA provides for non-discrimination in employee eligibility or continued eligibility to enroll for benefits under the terms of an employer group health plan without regard to health factors. If the employee was covered by the previous employer and maintained that coverage for 18 months, the new employer is required to offer the same healthcare benefits as are offered to other employees within the organization.

Under Title I, not only must employer group health plans not discriminate against any employee in the provision of healthcare benefits, but the employee may not be charged more for coverage than other persons under the same plan in the employer organization because of health status factors. While the group plan may exclude certain diseases from coverage, limit coverage benefits, and place lifetime limits on coverage, the plan must do the same for all "similarly situated individuals." It may not single out one group or individual for coverage limits due to the health factors of that group or employee. In other words, coverage must apply consistently across all covered individuals who are "similarly situated." (8)

Title II of HIPAA is the Administrative Simplification section of the act and is the more widely known part of the law because of its requirement for patient information privacy. Under Title II, the law provided for the prevention of healthcare fraud and abuse, reform of medical liability, and administrative simplification. The administrative simplification provision required the establishment of national standards for electronic health records (EHRs), and called for national identifiers for providers, employers, and health insurance plans. Under those provisions, healthcare providers are required to provide for the security of patient data and the protection of the privacy of electronic patient health information (e-PHI).

The HIPAA Security Rule compliance requirements for covered entities maintain that reasonable and appropriate administrative, technical and physical safeguards for protecting e-PHI

1. Ensure the confidentiality, integrity, and availability of all e-PHI they create, receive, maintain, or transmit;
2. Identify and protect against reasonably anticipated threats to the security or integrity of the information;
3. Protect against reasonably anticipated impermissible uses or disclosures; and
4. Ensure compliance by their workforce.

(9)

Healthcare organizations—including all healthcare providers, health plans, public health authorities, healthcare clearinghouses, and self-insured employers—as well as life insurers, information systems vendors, various service organizations, and universities that exchange healthcare data electronically are affected by HIPAA. It is a consequential requirement because noncompliance makes these organizations subject to both civil and criminal penalties. Fines for violations can range from $100 up to $50,000 and, for repeated offenses, penalties can be much higher. Criminal violations can incur imprisonment up to ten years for knowing misuse of individually identifiable health information.

7.2.9 Patient Protection and Affordable Care Act

The Patient Protection and Affordable Care Act is also known as the PPACA, ACA and Obamacare. Passed in 2010, it was the most significant change affecting healthcare insurance for Americans and shaping the U.S. healthcare system since the passage of Medicare and Medicaid in 1965. The ACA addressed a broad range of health insurance coverage issues, prominent among them:

- New insurance market regulations were imposed including prohibition of a pre-existing conditions period and of lifetime and annual limits on coverage, and a requirement for extension of dependent coverage to age 26.
- Requirement for coverage of ten essential health benefits in individual and small group plans, including ambulatory care, emergency care, maternity and newborn care, laboratory services, preventive care, chronic disease management, and more.
- Requirement for no-cost preventive care benefits and limited annual cost-sharing.
- Creation of state-based health insurance exchanges through which individuals could compare and purchase coverage.
- Provision of cost-sharing subsidies.
- Expansion of Medicaid eligibility to all non-elderly adults meeting defined income requirements.

(10)

Prior to 2012, more than 44 million Americans were uninsured and up to 129 million lacked coverage for pre-existing conditions, some of which were life threatening. By 2016, almost 20 more million people had healthcare coverage than prior to the passage of the ACA and limits on pre-existing conditions were no longer included in health insurance plans. (11) The ACA will be discussed further in Chapter 8.

7.3 Malpractice

Medical malpractice litigation, as explained by Studdert et al., has three social goals: "to deter unsafe practices, to compensate persons injured through negligence, and to exact corrective justice." (12) In the litigious society of the United States, the level of legal action against physicians and the tens and, in some instances, hundreds of millions of dollars in rewards given to plaintiffs have driven up the cost of malpractice insurance for physicians. On average annual malpractice insurance premiums can range up to $50,000 or more. In particular, Ob/GYNs may face premiums exceeding $200,000 in certain geographic areas.

During the 1990s, the United States experienced a particularly rapid increase in the cost of physician malpractice premiums, just as physician fees were being curbed under the Resource Based Relative Value Scale (RBRVS) and under managed care plans. Physicians found themselves not only in the dilemma of earning less revenue in their practices but also coping with rapidly rising costs of liability insurance. The "epidemic" of physician responses to counter the higher premiums drove some to leave the practice of medicine, others moved into new physician-related professions, and some others moved en masse out of certain states. The crises that resulted pushed states to find solutions, and different states took different courses of action. Some established their own state-operated malpractice insurance programs offering lower premiums to doctors. Other states undertook tort reform, establishing ceilings on the amount of damages that plaintiffs could be awarded in malpractice cases and on the amounts of fees paid to lawyers. For a number of years, these measures "cooled" the heightened concern of the 1990s; however, from time to time and from state to state or locality to locality, issues related to the costs of malpractice insurance continue to rise.

7.4 Summary

In this chapter, we have covered only a few of the major areas of legislation and other public policy initiatives that impact healthcare providers. While this gives an overview of key statutes, it is important to consider that each of these and other laws and regulations are frequently amended or clarified through the process of regulation, of judicial decisions, and of executive orders. Additionally, since the government is a major payer of healthcare services, policy is frequently made by line items in the budgets that Congress approves and in the modifications to those line items that happen in the executive administration of the budget. Line item changes in budget allocations can, for example, provide increased or decreased support for one service while conversely increasing or decreasing support for another service, such as hospice care or home healthcare. These are the changes that happen out of the sight of the legislature, yet they have significant impact on the people who rely on the benefits of governmental payment programs and on providers who care for patients.

References

1. R.K. Newman. *Hill–Burton Act (1946).* Available at www.encyclopedia.com/ history/encyclopedias-almanacs-transcripts-and-maps/hill-burton-act-1946.
2. Office of the Assistant Secretary for Planning and Evaluation, U.S. Department of Health and Human Services. *Poverty guidelines: 01/15/21.* Available at https://aspe.hhs.gov/poverty-guidelines.
3. Daily Briefing. Advisory Board. 2020 (Apr. 3). *CMS: US health care spending will reach $4T in 2020.* Available at www.advisory.com/daily-briefing/ 2020/04/03/health-spending#:~:text=CMS%20also%20estimated%20that%20 Medicare%20spending%20reached%20%24800.7,annual%20rate%20of%20 7.6%25%20from%202019%20to%202028.
4. Medicare.gov. *Medicare advantage plans.* Available at www.medicare.gov/ sign-up-change-plans/types-of-medicare-health-plans/medicare-advantage-plans.
5. R.F. Averill, N. Goldfield, J.S. Hughes, J. Bonazelli, E.C. McCullough, B.A. Steinbeck, R. Mullin, A.M. Tang, J. Muldoon, L. Turner and J. Gay. 2003. *All Patient Refined Diagnosis Related Groups (APR-DRGs): Methodology overview.* 3M Health Information Systems, Wallingford, CT.
6. Frequently asked questions about the emergency medical transfer and active labor act. Available at www.emtala.com/faq.htm.
7. K. Sandrick. 2008. Stark laws then and now. *Trustee,* 61(2): 33–35.
8. Health Insurance Portability and Accountability Act of 1996 (HIPAA). *Title I: Health care access, portability, and renewability.* Available at http://hipaa.ohio. gov/whitepapers/title1healthcareaccess.PDF. Accessed April 2002.
9. HHS.gov. *Summary of HIPAA security rule.* Available at www.hhs.gov/hipaa/ for-professionals/security/laws-regulations/index.html.
10. Kaiser Family Foundation. 2017 (Mar.). *Summary of the affordable care act.* Available at https://files.kff.org/attachment/Summary-of-the-Affordable-Care-Act.

11. R. Garfield, K. Orgero, A. Damico. Kaiser Family Foundation. 2019 (Jan. 25). *The uninsured and the ACA: A primer: Key facts about health insurance and the uninsured amidst changes to the Affordable Care Act.* Available at www. kff.org/report-section/the-uninsured-and-the-aca-a-primer-key-facts-about-health-insurance-and-the-uninsured-amidst-changes-to-the-affordable-care-act-how-many-people-are-uninsured/.
12. D.M. Studdert, M.M. Mello and T.A. Brennan. 2004. Medical malpractice. *New England Journal of Medicine,* 350: 283–292.

Chapter 8

Financing Healthcare

8.1 Introduction

Unlike other sectors of the U.S. economy, healthcare has a "third party" structure in which most consumers are, in part, sheltered from the cost of the healthcare services they receive and purchase. In the typical commercial transaction, the consumer decides what they want to buy and from whom. At the time of the purchase, the consumer pays the seller directly for the service or item. In healthcare, however, when the consumer needs a medical exam, test, or procedure and has healthcare insurance coverage, they are removed from payment for the transaction, or at least from most of the cost. There are three parties in the transaction: the consumer, the provider, and the payer/insurer. This places a high level of power in the hands of the payer and a part of their role is to manage the "perverse incentive" that the consumer and provider may otherwise have to use excess, unnecessary services. The payer has the power to establish parameters, such as pricing restrictions, on the use of services by each of the other two parties, the consumer and the provider. The consumer is not incentivized to save, but, to the contrary, has a personal well-being incentive to seek the best and often the most expensive care available. Consider the example of pharmaceuticals: a patient may want/demand a drug that they've learned about through advertising, and if that drug is the most expensive on the market even though comparable quality results can be achieved with a less expensive or generic drug, the physician is often incentivized to order the expensive drug because the patient will be happy. The third-party concept removes healthcare delivery from the norms of market forces that are meant to balance supply and demand for goods and services.

DOI: 10.4324/9781003202950-8

In the U.S., healthcare financing is provided primarily by two types of payers or insurers: public payers and private payers. Public payers include all government or tax supported healthcare insurance programs such as Medicare, Medicaid, the Veterans Health Administration, and the Indian Health Services. Private payers include commercial health insurers such as Blue Cross Blue Shield, Aetna, and others. In healthcare, the term "private payers" also includes consumers who pay out-of-pocket costs for all or a portion of the services they receive. Adding complexity to the healthcare financing arrangement is the structure in which employers provide health insurance coverage for their employees. In 2017, 56.0 percent of the U.S. population was covered by employer-based health insurance. This role gives employers authority in healthcare decisions in that they determine, within certain parameters, the medical tests and procedures that will be covered by their employee health insurance plans.

Financing of healthcare in the U.S. is a complex, multi-tiered system that supports the most expensive healthcare delivery system in the world. Despite the recent progress made under the PPACA, it leaves a significant portion of the population with no coverage and others with too little coverage. This engenders an expensive cost-shifting phenomenon in which costs for paying patients and insurers are increased by amounts not collected from the uninsured and underinsured. Their costs of care are included in the computation of the hospital's expenses and then, inherently, in the fees that are charged to other payers. In this chapter, we look at the cost of healthcare in the U.S. and the major payers who have the third-party role in covering that cost.

8.2 National Health Expenditures

The first place to start the discussion of healthcare costs is with a focus on healthcare expenditures and their distribution among the providers of care. As we ended 2019, the U.S. tab for healthcare (hospitals, physicians, pharmaceuticals, nursing home care, and so on) was $3.8 trillion or 17.7 percent of the gross domestic product (GDP). This was up from $790 billion in 1990 and $1.4 trillion in 2000 when the cost of healthcare in the U.S. represented 11 percent and 13.3 percent, respectively, of the gross domestic product (GDP). In 2019, national healthcare spending increased 4.6 percent over 2018 which was a higher rate than the 3.4 percent at which the U.S. economy grew. Average costs per capita in the U.S. in 2019 were $11,582 compared to $2,833 in 1990 and $4,843 in 2000 (see Table 8.1).

Of the total national health expenditures in 2019, 31 percent was paid to hospitals, physicians, and other clinical services accounted for 20 percent,

Table 8.1   U.S. Health Expenditures and GDP

	1990	*2000*	*2019*
Total U.S. health expenditures	$790B	$1.4T	$3.8T
Healthcare spending per capita	$2,833	$4,843	$11,582
U.S. average annual GDP growth	4.5%	2.9%	3.4%
National health expenditures as percent of GDP	11%	13.3%	17.7%

Source: R. Kamal, D. McDermott, G. Ramirez and C. Cox. 2020 (Dec. 23.). Peterson-Kaiser Family Foundation. *Health System Tracker.* Available at www.healthsystem-tracker.org/chart-collection/u-s-spending-healthcare-changed-time/

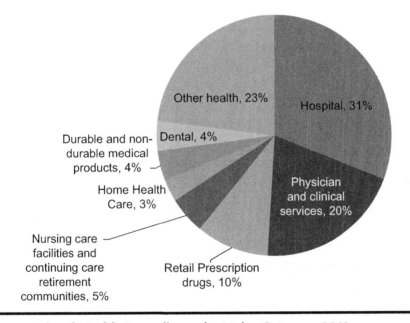

Figure 8.1 National Health Expenditures by Major Category, 2019

Source: Centers for Medicare & Medicaid Services, Office of the Actuary, National Health Statistics Group. Available at https://www.cms.gov/files/document/nations-health-dollar-where-it-came-where-it-went.pdf.

and nursing homes and continuing care retirement communities received 5 percent, while pharmaceuticals consumed 10 percent and home health services 3 percent (see Figure 8.1).

Figure 8.2 represents the major sources of funding for U.S. National Health Expenditures (NHE). The federal government accounts for approximately 35 percent of all expenditures and private health insurance provides 31 percent. Personal out-of-pocket payments accounted for about 11 percent of the source of NHE.

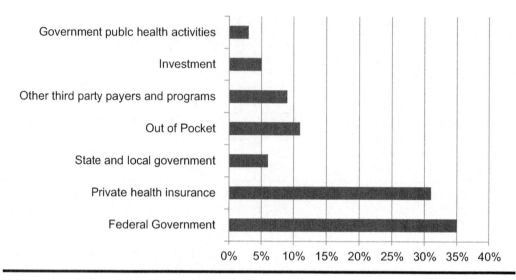

Figure 8.2 National Health Expenditures by Payer Source, 2019

Source: Centers for Medicare & Medicaid Services, Office of the Actuary, National Health Statistics Group. Available at https://www.cms.gov/files/document/nations-health-dollar-where-it-came-where-it-went.pdf

State and local governments are the payment source for 6 percent of NHE. State government costs relate primarily to their share of Medicaid, CHIP, mental health and addiction services, state prison system healthcare, employee insurance, and other medically related services within their constitutional responsibility. Much of the local government's share of the NHE relates to local public health services, medical care for jail populations, support of emergency services, and employee benefits. "Other private revenues" include expenditures in venues of care such as schools and certain non-traditional providers of care.

8.3 Medicare

Medicare was established under Title XVIII of the Social Security Amendments in 1963. At its outset, Medicare was created to finance care for the elderly, defined as persons aged 65 years or older. Subsequent to its passage, further legislation provided coverage for additional population groups including the disabled at any age and for persons with end-stage renal disease. Medicare provides coverage under four distinct parts, described in more detail in Figure 8.3:

- Part A, hospital insurance or HI, covers hospital, skilled nursing, home health, and hospice care

Part A: Hospital insurance

Helps pay for inpatient care in a hospital or skilled nursing facility (following a hospital stay), some home health care and hospice care.

Before age 65, you are eligible for free Medicare hospital insurance if:

You have been entitled to Social Security disability benefits for 24 months; or

You receive a disability pension from the railroad retirement board and meet certain conditions; or

You have Lou Gehrig's disease (amyotrophic lateral sclerosis); or

You worked long enough in a government job where Medicare taxes were paid and you meet the requirements of the Social Security disability program; or

You are the child or widow(er) age 50 or older, including a divorced widow(er), of someone who has worked long enough in a government job where Medicare taxes were paid and you meet the requirements of the Social Security disability program.

You have permanent kidney failure and you receive maintenance dialysis or a kidney transplant and:

— You are eligible for or receive monthly benefits under Social Security or the railroad retirement system; or

— You have worked long enough in a Medicare-covered government job; or

— You are the child or spouse (including a divorced spouse) of a worker (living or deceased) who has worked long enough under Social Security or in a Medicare-covered government job.

Part B: Medical insurance

Helps pay for doctors' services and many other medical services and supplies that are not covered by hospital insurance.

Anyone who is eligible for free Medicare hospital insurance (Part A) can enroll in Medicare medical insurance (Part B) by paying a monthly premium. Some beneficiaries with higher incomes will pay a higher monthly Part B premium.

If you are not eligible for free hospital insurance, you can buy medical insurance, without having to buy hospital insurance, if you are age 65 or older and you are—

A U.S. citizen; or

A lawfully admitted noncitizen who has lived in the United States for at least five years.

Part C: Medicare Advantage

Plans are available in many areas. People with Medicare Parts A and B can choose to receive all of their health care services through one of these provider organizations under Part C.

If you have Medicare Parts A and B, you can join a Medicare Advantage plan. With one of these plans, you do not need a Medigap policy, because Medicare Advantage plans generally cover many of the same benefits that a Medigap policy would cover, such as extra days in the hospital after you have used the number of days that Medicare covers.

Medicare Advantage plans include:

Medicare managed care plans;

Medicare preferred provider organization (PPO) plans;

Medicare private fee-for-service plans; and

Medicare specialty plans.

If you decide to join a Medicare Advantage plan, you use the health card that you get from your Medicare Advantage plan provider for your health care. Also, you might have to pay a monthly premium for your Medicare Advantage plan because of the extra benefits it offers.

Part D: Prescription drug coverage

Helps pay for medications doctors prescribe for treatment.

Anyone who has Medicare hospital insurance (Part A), medical insurance (Part B), or a Medicare Advantage plan (Part C) is eligible for prescription drug coverage (Part D). Joining a Medicare prescription drug plan is voluntary, and you pay an additional monthly premium for the coverage. You can wait to enroll in a Medicare Part D plan if you have other prescription drug coverage but, if you don't have prescription coverage that is, on average, at least as good as Medicare prescription drug coverage, you will pay a penalty if you wait to join later. You will have to pay this penalty for as long as you have Medicare prescription drug coverage.

Figure 8.3 Medicare Parts A-B-C-D.

Source: Social Security Administration. SSA Publication No. 05-10043, ICN 460000. May 2008. http://www.ssa.gov/pubs/10043.pdf

- Part B, medical insurance, pays for physician services and other medical services and supplies
- Part C provides the enrollee coverage through Medicare Advantage managed care plans
- Part D provides prescription coverage.

Originally, Medicare consisted only of Parts A and B. Part A is paid for from the Medicare Trust Fund which is financed by general tax revenues. Medicare requires payment of premiums for Part B and of deductibles and co-payments for medical services rendered under both Parts A and B. These coverage co-payments and deductibles are also known as gaps in coverage or "medigaps." To cover the cost of these gaps, the enrollee can purchase Medicare supplemental insurance, i.e., medigap or supplemental insurance, from insurer plans that are approved under federal guidelines.

Medicare was born out of the 1945 vision of President Harry Truman when he proposed that the United States institute a universal healthcare program. Strongly opposed by the American Medical Association, it was not until after Lyndon Johnson took office that legislation would be approved by Congress as "Medicare" and signed by the President.

Administratively, Medicare was placed under the operational control of the Health Care Financing Administration within the Department of Health, Education, and Welfare. These offices later evolved into the current Centers for Medicare and Medicaid Services (CMS) within the Department of Health and Human Services.

8.3.1 Medicare Cost Control Initiatives

Over the years since the inception of Medicare, a number of major initiatives have been taken to reduce the rate of increase in Medicare costs. In an early major initiative, the Health Resources and Development Act of 1974 was enacted establishing State-wide hospital planning and Certificate of Need (CON) programs in an attempt to control capital expenditures (discussed in Chapter 7). The rate of increase in national healthcare costs did not abate, and in a further effort to curb rising healthcare costs and to keep Medicare and Medicaid from insolvency, the mid-1980s saw the development of the *prospective payment system* (PPS). Policy makers

> turned to the one alternative reimbursement system that analysts and academics had studied more than any other and had even

tested with apparent success in New Jersey: prospective payment with diagnosis-related groups (DRGs). Rather than simply reimbursing hospitals whatever costs they charged to treat Medicare patients, the new model paid hospitals a predetermined, set rate based on the patient's diagnosis. . . . [PPS is described as] the most significant change in health policy since Medicare and Medicaid's passage in 1965 . . . and which went virtually unnoticed by the general public.

(1)

Initially, PPS was legislated and implemented with a primary focus on providers of inpatient acute care. As discussed in Chapter 7, this generated a major shift of volume and costs from inpatient services to ambulatory facilities. In 1980, about three million surgical procedures were done in the hospital-based and independent ambulatory setting, by 1995, that number was 27 million. (2) In the following decade, the number of inpatient admissions again increased and by 2014, the numbers of inpatient and outpatient surgical procedures were almost equal to one another. In surgical procedures alone, by 2014, about 11.5 million surgeries or 52.7 percent were performed in a hospital-based ambulatory setting, and just over 10.3 million or 47.3 percent were done in an inpatient setting. (3) For a few years after the implementation of PPS, the country saw a general slowing in the rate of increase in national healthcare expenditures, but the slowdown didn't last long, and health expenditures picked up to a rapid pace of increase again. More than a decade after the inception of the inpatient PPS, the majority of other providers of care (ambulatory care, long-term nursing facilities, rehabilitation care) came under the prospective payment reimbursement structure in a further effort to control national healthcare expenditures.

Four additional major areas in which CMS has focused Medicare cost-control policy are:

■ To control *fraud and abuse*, CMS has used the long-established Anti-Kickback Statute, Stark I and Stark II/Self-Referral Law/Limitations on Certain Physician Referrals and the Federal Civil False Claims Act to address issues as they arise, particularly in Medicare reimbursement. Under the Stark rules, physicians are prohibited from referring patients to other provider and service entities (e.g., labs) in which they have a financial interest.

■ Under the Medicare Prescription Drug, Improvement and Modernization Act of 2003, CMS was authorized to launch the Recovery Audit Contractor (RAC) program. Because reimbursements are made to providers based on the code assigned to the patient diagnosis, a pattern of "upcoding" was suspected, as well as the probability of unintentional errors in coding. The RAC program was designed to more aggressively seek out billing and coding errors (whether intentional or not) that cause overpayments or underpayments to providers. Under this program, auditors go into hospitals to review their billing processes and documents in order to determine whether or not coding of diagnosis and treatments was correct. Where errors are found, the hospital is required to compensate the Medicare program for the difference or if the error is one in which the hospital was paid too little, the Medicare program reimburses the added amount to the hospital. In 2018, the RAC program found approximately $89 million in overpayments to providers. (4)

■ Regarding *quality of care*, CMS began in 2001 to initiate programs that would promote and foster healthcare quality improvement through public disclosure of information and holding providers to accountable standards of care. Strategies used by CMS to implement quality improvement include payment incentives to providers, payment reductions when disincentives are needed and public reporting on healthcare quality performance through government websites such as www.medicare.gov/care-compare. Payment reductions were initiated through policies such as stopping reimbursement for the cost of correcting medical errors that are preventable. These "never events" include preventable errors such as wrong-site surgery or administration of wrong blood types (these are discussed further in Chapter 9).

■ In 2015, a bipartisan Congress passed the Medicare Access and CHIP Re-authorization Act (MACRA) to reform the Medicare payment system, particularly for physicians. Under the Act, the Medicare Physician Fee Schedule was updated with a value-based payment system. The prior formula used an SGR or sustainable growth rate in the formula for physician payment. This cost control initiative attempted to ensure that the annual cost increase in expense per Medicare enrollee did not exceed the growth in GDP, in other words, spending on physician services for Medicare patients would be more stringently controlled. Physicians would experience significant decrease in their income, and many threatened to leave the Medicare program if the SGR were implemented. Congress delayed implementation of the formula each year from 2002 to 2015, until it was finally eliminated and replaced with a value-based measure in 2015. MACRA requires CMS to establish value-based physician payment models that tie a constantly increasing portion of physician payments to service-value instead of service-volume.

(5)

8.3.2 *The Sustainability of Medicare*

The financial viability or sustainability of Medicare is the subject of much ongoing debate and analysis. Medicare was designed as a program that would be funded through two funds:

■ The Medicare Trust Fund which is financed primarily through payroll taxes and income taxes on Social Security benefits. The trust fund pays for stays in hospitals, skilled nursing facilities and hospices under Part A.
■ The Supplemental Medical Insurance Fund which is financed by general tax revenues and premium payments by enrollees for Part B services. This includes physician visits and medical supplies and Part D that covers prescription drugs.

Because of the funding mechanism for Medicare, there is an inherent shift of short-term wealth from the younger population to the senior enrollees. From the start in the 1960s, persons age 65 and over were enrolled in Medicare while the employed population paid into the system with the "promise" that they would also have coverage under Medicare when they turned age 65. However, payments into the system have not kept pace with the rate of healthcare cost inflation. Over the intervening decades between the 1960s and the turn of the century, the demographics of the working population and the elderly population shifted. In the decades since the 1960s, the working population of baby boomers has increasingly outstripped the numbers of the elderly or retired and, consequently, there have been, and are, proportionately fewer and fewer people paying into the fund while more and more turn age 65 and become entitled to Medicare enrollment. As baby boomers have retired, the pressure on the Medicare Trust

Fund has intensified as has concern about the viability of Medicare and the need for a fundamental approach to restructuring the program in order to avoid its bankruptcy.

To explain a bit more about how the Medicare Trust Funds works. A Kaiser Foundation brief explains it this way:

> Operationally, Medicare financing is managed through two trust fund accounts. The Hospital Insurance (HI) Trust Fund, into which Medicare payroll taxes and other dedicated revenue are credited, pays for inpatient hospital stays and other benefits provided under Medicare Part A. In 2006, the payroll tax provided 86 percent of all the revenue attributed to the HI Trust Fund, and 42 percent of Medicare revenue overall. The Supplementary Medical Insurance (SMI) Trust Fund is used to pay for physician visits and other Medicare Part B services as well as the Medicare Part D pre-scription drug benefit. The SMI Trust Fund is financed primarily through monthly beneficiary Part B premiums, prescription drug plan premiums, and general revenue.
>
> (6)

8.4 Medicaid

Medicaid was established in 1963 concurrently with Medicare and under Title XIX of the Social Security Amendments. Medicaid provides healthcare coverage to persons who are indigent and who are eligible for coverage based on specific criteria related to their income level.

Medicaid is a means-tested entitlement program that finances primary and acute care services and long-term care. Medicaid covers some low-income populations, including pregnant women, children and adults with diverse physical and mental health conditions and disabilities, and indigent elderly and disabled Medicare beneficiaries. Eligibility varies among states because, while states must meet federal minimum requirements, they may also choose to cover additional optional populations.

The PPACA, or ACA, extended coverage to qualifying non-disabled adults without children in those states that agreed to extend coverage to these populations. 38 states have done so. (7) The ACA also included provisions that required eligibility, enrollment and renewal processes be streamlined in all states whether or not they participated in the ACA expansion of coverage provisions to all qualifying adults. With these changes in particular, enrollment and spending increased across the board.

In its overall scope, in 2020 Medicaid and CHIP expenditures were estimated to be approximately $683 billion and covered 71.4 million enrollees. (7) This was up from 2010 when Medicaid paid over $400 billion and provided coverage for approximately 65.7 million enrollees.

8.4.1 *Federal/State Medicaid Matching Funding*

Federal law provides that states may qualify for federal Medicaid matching funds if the program is designed within specific federal requirements. These include eligibility for defined population groups, coverage for certain medical services and medical providers, and adherence to rules relating to payment methodologies, payment amounts, and cost sharing for Medicaid beneficiaries. States also have the authority to extend Medicaid benefits beyond the minimum federally established standards. Under these provisions, Medicaid eligibility and coverage provisions vary from state to state.

Two key criteria are used to derive the level of federal matching funds for which a state is eligible under Medicaid: (1) the actual amount spent for services for enrollees that qualify as eligible for federal matching funds under Medicaid and (2) the federal medical assistance percentage (FMAP). The FMAP is computed on the average per capita income for the state relative to the national average. By law, the FMAP cannot be less than 50 percent of the state's Medicaid budget; in other words, the federal government pays at least one-half of the state's Medicaid budget. States with per capita personal incomes below the national average can receive matching levels up to 78 percent of their costs (e.g., Mississippi has been federally funded at this level). (8) In addition to matching funds for the direct cost of care received by enrollees, states receive matching funds for the administrative operation of their programs. Generally, this rate is set at 50 percent of cost, although it may be higher under certain circumstances such as for those activities requiring skilled professionals.

8.4.2 *Waivers*

Certain programmatic requirements are placed on states in order to participate in Medicaid. These include provisions that Medicaid beneficiaries have freedom of choice of providers, that the program is offered statewide, and that services are adequately available in volume, duration, and scope to achieve their goals. Beyond this, the federal Medicaid law also allows waivers from statutory requirements so that a state can design its program to meet the unique needs of the state or to bring innovative efficiencies to the program. The CMS may grant "program waivers" or "research and demonstration waivers." Waivers have been used, for example, in the creation of state Medicaid managed care programs.

8.4.3 Medicaid Managed Care

Increasingly, Medicaid programs have moved toward the use of managed care arrangements. Managed care is an approach to healthcare delivery in which the provider organization has systems in place to manage the cost, utilization, and quality of services. Under these programs, states contract with managed care organizations (MCOs) that accept a defined per-member-per-month capitation payment for services needed by the Medicaid enrollees. The MCO is required to have an adequate range of primary and specialty care services available to meet the needs of the defined population base. Under the MCO arrangement, the beneficiary selects a specific primary care provider in the MCO's network who is then responsible for providing and authorizing needed medical care. The MCO is responsible to have an adequate range of services, including specialties and clinicians, in a given geographic area to ensure the beneficiaries can access the services they need. The patient has access to care through the primary care provider and their care is managed for reduced redundancy (e.g., duplication of tests), quality assurance, and reduced costs.

8.5 Children's Health Insurance Program

The State Children's Health Insurance Program (SCHIP or CHIP) was initiated under Title XXI of the Social Security Act as part of the Balanced Budget Act of 1997. CHIP was designed to build on Medicaid to provide insurance coverage to targeted low-income children who are uninsured and not eligible for Medicaid.

Many parents work in minimum or low-wage jobs and do so without the benefit of employer-provided health insurance for their families or the ability to financially afford to pay the cost of health insurance premiums. While many of these families support their households, their children may go without healthcare coverage due to its prohibitive cost. CHIP provides the opportunity for them to have that coverage.

CHIP is operational under state Medicaid programs and provides healthcare coverage to eligible children. It is funded through a partnership of the states and the federal government. The federal government's matching CHIP funding is set at a higher percentage than it is under Medicaid. Additionally, eligibility for children is established at a higher poverty level for families than the Medicaid program. Children who are covered under Medicaid are not eligible for CHIP.

While states determine the coverage provided to their residents, the federal minimum income participation parameters are that the poverty level range for a family's income must be between 170 percent and 400 percent of the Federal poverty level (FPL). The program applies to children under 19 years of age who are uninsured, are citizens or meet immigration requirements, reside in the state, and are eligible within the state's CHIP family income poverty level range.

8.6 Other Governmentally Financed Healthcare Programs

In addition to Medicare, Medicaid, and CHIP, the federal government provides several other health insurance programs for citizens of the United States. Prominent among these are the programs offered by the U.S. Department of Veterans Affairs (VA), Tricare and the Indian Health Service (IHS).

8.6.1 *Military Healthcare Programs*

Within the VA is the Department of Veterans Health Administration, which provides healthcare services to retired military personnel. The VA operates 1,293 healthcare facilities including 171 medical centers and 1,112 outpatient clinics serving over nine million veterans. According to the U.S. Department of Veterans Affairs, the VA is viewed as being a fully networked system, tied together with information technology that supports input and access to patient medical information without geographic constraints. In 2020, the Veterans Health Administration budget was $80.2 billion or about 40 percent the total VA budget. (9)

Tricare, formerly known as the Civil Health and Medical Program for the Uniformed Services (CHAMPUS), provides medical care for active and retired members of the military and their families, military retirees, and their dependents. Tricare is the civilian component of the military health system. It operates under the authority of the U.S. Department of Defense Military Health System and is directly managed by the Defense Health Agency. In 2020, the Military Health System budget was set at $49.5 billion to provide services to approximately 9.6 million beneficiaries.

8.6.2 *Indian Health Service*

The Indian Health Services (IHS) is also fully funded by the federal government and provides both inpatient and outpatient services to Native Americans and Alaska Eskimo tribe members through pacts that have been in place between the U.S. federal government and the governing councils of the tribes since 1787. In that year, this relationship was established and was codified in Article 1, Section 8, of the Constitution. The IHS currently has 46 hospitals and over 300 health centers as well as health stations, Alaska village clinics, school health centers, and youth regional treatment centers. With a budget in 2020 of $6 billion these services provide care to approximately 2.6 million American Indians and Alaska Natives who belong to more than 574 federally recognized tribes in 37 states. (10)

8.7 The Private Sector in Healthcare Financing

While governmental agencies represent about 45 percent of funding of healthcare in the U.S., over 50 percent of overall healthcare financing comes from private sources. These include employer-sponsored healthcare coverage, out-of-pocket payments for medical services by individuals, and individually purchased private health insurance premiums. Given the dominance of various kinds of governmental and private insurance coverage programs that are available in the U.S., households still carry a large portion of the burden of healthcare costs in out-of-pocket payments. As shown in Figure 8.2, out-of-pocket, i.e., household, payments as a portion of National Health Expenditures (NHE) was 28 percent in 2019, or more than a quarter. These household expenditures include the employee share of employer provided insurance, enrollee premiums for Medicare Parts B and D, deductibles and co-payments, and purchases of drugs and medical services that are not covered partially or in full by insurance.

8.7.1 *Employer Health Insurance Plans*

The opportunity for employer-sponsored health insurance originated in several initiatives that were evolving among employers in the United States in the first decades of the twentieth century. For example, in Chicago, Montgomery Ward offered a new insurance policy to its employees in 1912. The program was primarily a life insurance policy, but it also included health and disability benefits.

The major thrust in the implementation of health insurance occurred in Dallas in 1929 when the superintendent of schools, Justin Ford Kimball, was hired by Baylor University as vice president in charge of the Baylor University College of Medicine, School of Nursing, and Baylor Hospital. In an initiative to bolster the financial performance of the university hospital, Kimball created a program for the Dallas school teachers in which each teacher paid $.50 a month to fund hospital care for any of them should they need it. This plan was designed as a prepaid health plan in which the hospital assumed risk for the medical care of the teachers. While the teachers agreed to pay a $.50 monthly premium, the hospital entered into this arrangement with data that indicated that, on average, teachers' healthcare costs had been about $.15 per month. With this data in hand, the hospital was willing to assume the risk of potential catastrophic need among one or more of the teachers whose medical care would cost the hospital more. The plan was successful and that message quickly spread across the country. Other provider organizations began to organize prepaid plans under the aegis of the American Hospital Association. Sharing a common purpose, they used a blue cross as the insignia or "brand" for the offering and this "symbol, in turn, led to a common name"–Blue Cross (11). Employers began financing healthcare insurance as an employee benefit in the World War II era.

Prior to the 1990s, employers offered health insurance plans to their employees, but paid minimal attention to how much health insurers were paying for medical care. Based on those payouts, insurers raised premiums to employers as needed to cover employee medical costs. However, as health insurance costs increased rapidly, employers became more aware of the impact of employee healthcare insurance on their financial performance. To manage these costs they turned to managed care organizations (MCOs) in the early 1990s to negotiate with providers for discounted rates. Included in the discounted rate contracts was a provision under which the MCO was authorized to employ a managed care function to review and approve medical services provided to covered employees and their family members prior to payment. As a result managed care gained a significant role in determining the medical services that would be provided to an insured person and in influencing medical decision making. This persists to the present time as MCOs use payment and outcomes data to determine services and treatments that they will and will not cover.

Today, employer coverage continues to morph as employers look for more effective ways of reducing the burden of healthcare coverage on their bottom lines. Plans that engage the employee more extensively in paying for coverage and that offer incentives for employees to engage in healthy behaviors have been implemented. In these strategies, employers attempt to place more responsibility on the employee to make considered and cost-conscious decisions in medical care. Employers also design wellness programs to reduce the cost of healthcare coverage. e.g., smoking cessation, weight loss, and exercise. Employees participating in these programs are typically offered financial incentives for achieving agreed-upon goals.

A number of U.S. employers offer consumer-driven healthcare plans in the form of high deductible health plans (HDHPs) that are tied to health savings accounts (HSAs). In these plans, the employer pays into the HSA in amounts that equal or approximate the plan's high deductible and the employee contributes pre-tax income to the HSA. Those funds are then available for medical deductibles, co-payments, and services during the year. Any funds remaining in the HSA after healthcare costs are paid in a given year are rolled over to the next year. The principle behind HSAs is that the employee will be incentivized to make good healthcare decisions because any savings in the account belong to the employee.

8.8 Managed Care Organizations (MCOs)

Managed care, as discussed earlier, is a system in which a health insurance or related company forms or owns an entity that can influence the type and level of healthcare services that patients consume and from whom they receive care. MCOs establish quality criteria and metrics in order to manage and coordinate the patients' care and thereby limit costs while ensuring quality processes and outcomes. Under some managed care programs, patients must choose their providers from within a network of providers with whom the managed care organization (MCO) has contracted for services at negotiated fees. Patients who get medical care from a provider outside the network may pay the full cost of the service or a much higher co-payment than they would pay to providers in the network. Providers within the network are monitored and assessed for quality indicators.

Some of the cost control mechanisms used by MCOs include choice restriction, case management, utilization review, and practice profiling.

Choice restriction: This is the limitation placed on members in their choice of providers. Typically, managed care plans contract with a network of providers, and in that contract, both parties agree to a discounted fees for the services that the provider offers. By limiting the number of providers in the network, the managed care plan can offer higher volume business to the provider, in exchange for which the provider is willing to reduce his or her fees.

Case management: Case management requires an arrangement in which a nurse or other trained clinician follows the patient to ensure compliance with treatment regimens. The patient's compliance with treatment regimens has been found to prevent the escalation of a medical condition to acute episodes that threaten the patient's well-being and can be excessively costly. Case management protocols are established to assess the needs and values of the patient. Following the assessment, the case manager connects clients with appropriate providers and resources throughout the continuum of health and human services and care settings. A key role of the case manager is ensuring that the care provided is safe, effective, client-centered, timely, efficient, and equitable.

Utilization review: This is a mechanism through which provider and physician practice patterns are assessed. In performing a utilization review, the managed care company, or the hospital, considers the diagnosis on which a patient is admitted for care, continuously analyzes the reasons for which the patient is hospitalized, and anticipates a projected date of the patient's discharge from the hospital.

There are a number of structures under which managed care organizations are structured. Common types of MCOs are:

Health Maintenance Organization (HMO): An HMO is a comprehensive healthcare financing and delivery organization that is inclusive of the roles of insurer and provider of care. HMOs provide or arrange for the provision of healthcare services to enrollees within a geographical

7

area through a panel of providers, including hospitals, ambulatory centers, and other venues of care. Typical models within an HMO include staff models and group models. A staff model HMO provides medical care through salaried physician employees. The group model HMO delivers care through a contract with one or more medical group practices. Both of these models typically function under a capitated arrangement, meaning they are paid established rates on a per-member-per-month basis and must deliver needed services regardless of the number of members who present for medical care. HMOs can also be operated under an independent practice association, in which a panel of physician providers contract as a group for their services.

Preferred provider organization (PPO): A PPO offers a variety of health plans that are accountable to purchasers for cost, quality, access, and other services. Hospitals, physicians, and ancillary providers may be part of a PPO. The PPO negotiates discounts with providers to make their services available to PPO members. A PPO is a combination of a fee-for-service plan and an HMO.

Point of service (POS) plan: POS plans allow members to choose how and by whom healthcare services are delivered at the time they are needed; it gives them the choice of going outside an approved network of providers to seek care. POS provisions may be included in HMO, PPO, or fee-for-service plans. Under them, if a member seeks care outside the network, the payer will provide some coverage of the cost of that service, albeit at a lower level than the cost of an in-network provider. The member is required to pay a higher portion of the cost, which he or she is often willing to do in order to see the provider of choice. POS plans expand the members' range of choice of providers.

8.9 Fee-for-Service

A fee-for-service insurance plan is one in which fees paid to the physician or other provider are based on the services rendered. As with most insurance plans, the plan pays a portion of the fee and the patient pays the remainder in the form of a deductible or co-payment. While this type of plan generally offers freedom of choice of provider for the patients, it is usually more expensive as the payment is structured on the quantity of services and the potential for the provider to be incentivized to perform more services than needed.

As reimbursement models change, they are increasingly shifting away from the fee-for-service model to models that incentivize improved outcomes and increased efficiency in choice of diagnostic and treatment procedures.

8.10 PPACA

The Patient Protection and Affordable Care Act (PL 111-148) was signed into law on March 23, 2010. Also known as the ACA and Obamacare, the Act ushered in transformational change in healthcare that is more impactful than any experienced in the United States since the introduction of Medicare over 50 years ago. The intent of the PPACA is to expand healthcare coverage for the millions of uninsured in the country, to establish mechanisms to control the rate of increase in the cost of healthcare, and to improve healthcare delivery and outcomes of care.

In its goal to expand healthcare coverage, the ACA expanded Medicaid healthcare coverage for the uninsured who were living below the Federal poverty level. Previously Medicaid covered specific categories of individuals (i.e., low-income children, pregnant women, elderly and disabled individuals, and some parents) but excluded other low-income adults. Under the ACA, states have the option to not participate in the Medicaid expansion program, and as of late 2020, 12 states had declined participation. States that participate in the expansion are required to cover all low-income individuals who are at or below 138 percent of the poverty level. The ACA also made it easier for individuals to enroll in the Medicaid program in all states through modernized and simplified processes. It expanded the outreach of the Medicaid program in order to reach more people. By 2018 20.8 million people had been enrolled in insurance programs as a result of the ACA and among that number Medicaid and CHIP enrollments increased by 4.8 million people. (12) The ACA also expanded coverage for persons with pre-existing conditions by requiring that insurers could no longer deny coverage of their insured for pre-existing conditions.

In addition to expanding healthcare coverage, the ACA called for changes in the way in which healthcare is paid for and delivered. For example:

■ The ACA ushered in reductions in hospital payments under the traditional Medicare program and in payments to Medicare Advantage plans. This resulted in lower rates of increase in Medicare costs since the law was implemented.

■ It created mechanisms to reward or penalize some hospitals in the fee-for-service payment structure. Initiatives such as the value-based Hospital Readmission Reduction Program in which hospitals receive lower payments for inpatient admissions that happen within a short time after a prior discharge for the same diagnosis, and the Hospital-Acquired Condition Reduction Program in which hospitals receive lower payments to correct an avoidable medical error that results in a longer stay and added costs (e.g., a hospital-acquired infection).

■ The ACA also created provisions for healthcare providers to voluntarily form Accountable Care Organizations under which they agree to take responsibility for the costs and quality of care for a defined population.

After the ACA was passed, healthcare per capita prices rose by only 3.6 percent annually from 2010 to 2018 which is the slowest rate of increase in 50 years. However, over the following years after it was passed, opponents to the legislation brought legal challenges to the ACA. Most of these challenges were ultimately denied by the Supreme Court, but in 2012, the Court found in *NFIB v. Sebilius* that Congress lacked the constitutional authority to enact the individual mandate. In the alternative, the Court found that Congress could impose a tax on people who failed to comply. In 2017, Congress reduced the amount of the tax penalty to zero.

8.11 Healthcare Reform Options

In the United States, the public is barraged from time to time with possible public policy proposals that would change and restructure the way in which healthcare coverage is paid. Those initiatives range from a single-payer system, to a national health insurance program, to a national health system to any combination or feature of these. It is important to understand the distinctions between these options,

■ *National health insurance programs* are those in which the federal government provides for payment of medical care for all eligible citizens. The medical providers in national health insurance systems are organized under private auspices and/or local governments. In the United States, Medicare and Medicaid are examples of national health insurance programs in that they provide coverage for defined segments of the population. National health insurance programs may be funded through a variety of arrangements, including private/public arrangement in which an employer or consumer provides a portion of funding, regional or local government funding, and/or federal funding. Examples of national health insurance programs are those in Germany and Belgium where both taxation and employer contributions fund a payment program that is administered by an arm of the federal government.

■ *National Health System (NHS).* In a national health system, the government "owns" both the provision of medical services and the financing of those services. In other words, hospitals and other medical facilities are owned by the government and physicians, other clinicians and administrative staff are employed by the government. The UK offers an example of a national health system, however, over time, the UK has permitted private doctors and hospitals to operate as part of the healthcare infrastructure in the country.

■ *"Socialized medicine"* programs are those in which either taxation or compulsory contributions fund national healthcare services. This fund is administered by the government, and the government specifies what services will be covered. In the United States, the term "socialized medicine" is often used as a pejorative for national health insurance or a national health system, though neither of the latter is "socialized medicine" in the full definition of the term.

8.12 Summary

The financing of healthcare in the United States involves a complicated mix of public and private payers and of a wide array of payment arrangements, discounted fees, patient financial responsibility, and lack of financial coverage for medical services. Over the past decades, the rate of increase in healthcare costs has been indomitable–strategies and legislative initiatives have not conquered that rate of increase. It now consumes 17 percent of the U.S. GDP and is expected to consume 20 percent in the near future. Current approaches of consumer-directed health plans shift more of the cost to the patient. This has been shown to have some effect on consumer behavior in use of medical services. While more people are covered under the ACA, there are still millions of people who are left without coverage. Understanding the basics of the various approaches to financing healthcare that are at play in the United States is key to understanding how the healthcare provider functions and how priorities get established.

References

1. R. Mayes. 2007 (Jan). The origins, development, and passage of Medicare's revolutionary prospective payment system. *J Hist Med Allied Sci*, 62(1): 21–55. doi: 10.1093/jhmas/jrj038. PMID: 16467485. Available at https://pubmed.ncbi.nlm.nih.gov/16467485/.
2. L.J. Kozak, E. McCarthy and R. Pokras. 1999 (Fall). Changing patterns of surgical care in the United States, 1980–1995. *Health Care Financing Review*, 21(1): 31–39. Available at www.ncbi.nlm.nih.gov/pmc/articles/PMC4194612/.
3. C.A. Steiner, Z. Karaca, B.J. Moore, M.C. Imshaug and G. Pickens. 2017 (May). *Surgeries in hospital-based ambulatory surgery and hospital inpatient settings, 2014*. Available at www.hcup-us.ahrq.gov/reports/statbriefs/sb223-Ambulatory-Inpatient-Surgeries-2014.jsp. Revised July 2020.
4. J. LaPointe. 2019 (May 3). Recovery audit contractor reform eases provider burden, CMS says. *RevCycle Intelligence*. Available at https://revcycleintelligence.com/news/recovery-audit-contractor-reform-eases-provider-burden-cms-says#:~:text=May%2003%2C%202019%20-%20The%20Medicare%20fee-for-service%20Recovery,Verma%20reports%20in%20a%20new%20official%20blog%20post.
5. AAPC. *What is MACRA?* Available at www.aapc.com/macra/macra.aspx.
6. L. Potetz. 2008. *Financing medicare: An issue brief.* The Henry J. Kaiser Family Foundation. Available at www.kff.org/wp-content/uploads/2013/01/7731.pdf.
7. Centers for Medicare and Medicaid Services. 2020 (Feb.). *Medicaid and CHIP beneficiaries at a glance*. Available at www.medicaid.gov/medicaid/quality-of-care/downloads/beneficiary-ataglance.pdf.
8. Peter G. Peterson Foundation. 2021 (Jan. 21). *Budget basics: Medicaid*. www.pgpf.org/budget-basics/budget-explainer-medicaid.
9. L. Shane. 2019 (Dec. 19). Another big boost for VA funding in latest federal budget deal. *Military Times*. Available at www.militarytimes.com/news/pentagon-congress/2019/12/19/another-big-boost-for-va-funding-in-latest-federal-budget-deal/#:~:text=The%20bill%20includes%20%2480.2%20billion%20for%20the%20Veterans,women%20and%20%24300%20million%20in%20rural%20health%20initiatives.
10. Indian Health Services. *About IHS*. Available at www.ihs.gov/aboutihs/.
11. J. Asplund. 1998 (Feb. 23). Birth of the blues. *AHA News*, p. 8.
12. T. Sullivan. 2018 (May 6). HHS releases new ACA figures: 8 million individuals enrolled during the first period. *Policy and Medicine*. Available at www.policymed.com/2014/05/hhs-releases-new-aca-figures-8-million-individuals-enrolled-during-the-first-period.html.

Chapter 9

Quality

9.1 Introduction

Historically, quality improvement initiatives in healthcare can be traced back to the efforts of Florence Nightingale during and following the civil war and to the work of Ernest Codman a surgeon in Boston at the turn of the twentieth century. Dr. Codman, to the consternation and disapproval of many of his colleagues, studied medical outcomes in surgery and advocated for improved "end results." During the early and mid-twentieth century several individuals such as W. Edward Deming and Avedis Donabedian became leaders in process improvement and through their work brought a focus on ways to improve quality in healthcare. In the latter part of the century, the Health Care Financing Administration (HCFA), which was later name the Centers for Medicare and Medicaid Services (CMS), focused on the measurement and reporting of outcomes and processes as broad areas for evaluating quality in medical care. In 1987, HCFA released hospital-specific mortality data. This raised controversy about public reporting of healthcare data, and it generated resistance among hospitals to participate in providing that data. These federal and other initiatives, led the way to a watershed event for quality improvement when the Institute of Medicine (IOM) published its report on mortality outcomes in medical care in 1999.

In that year, the IOM publicly released a study entitled *To Err is Human* that reported credible evidence of tens of thousands of preventable deaths in hospitals annually. These deaths were caused by preventable errors–errors in drug and IV dosage; in medication administration; by wrong-site surgery (e.g., performing a surgical procedure on the patient's right knee when the left needed the surgery); by equipment malfunction; and by hospital-induced

DOI: 10.4324/9781003202950-9

infections from improper, or ignored, infection control processes such as hand washing and handling of catheters. Prior to the report professionals in healthcare were reticent to acknowledge occurrence of the patient care errors that were being noted anecdotally in patient charts. The IOM's report, however, seared into the minds of clinicians and management the startling news–as many as 98,000 people were dying in U.S. hospitals each year as a result of preventable errors. The numbers rose higher when the analysis of outcomes was expanded to include adverse events that did not lead to death. The cost of medical errors is not only in dollars and deaths, but also in the long-term impact on patients' lives for those who are faced with ongoing physical, mental, or emotional issues as well as added costs and lost productivity. (More on the IOM report later.)

In this chapter, we address some of the major initiatives that have been undertaken to improve quality and prevent medical errors. We will see that the focus is on measurement, standardization, process improvement, implementation of information and clinical technologies, and the design of new operational policies and, of course, education and continuous assessment.

9.2 Defining Quality in Healthcare

The Institute of Medicine defines healthcare quality as "the degree to which health services for individuals and populations increase the likelihood of desired health outcomes and are consistent with current professional knowledge." (1)

In healthcare, quality is viewed through different lenses by its varied participants: patients, clinicians, administrators, payers (including government), and employers.

- Patients typically view quality as related to the quality of their interpersonal interaction with the clinicians involved in their care and the environment of that care. When asked, they will often refer to the way in which the doctor or nurse talked to them, whether or not they feel that their situation got the attention it should get, the cleanliness of the clinical surroundings, and so on. Ultimately, as patients progress through the cure and healing processes, their perspective turns to outcomes.
- Physicians tend to define quality based on the outcomes of their care. They ask: Did the patient get well? Was the procedure done correctly?

They are scientists and want to know that their knowledge and skill resolved the medical issue with which they were presented.

■ Administrators view quality in part through the lens of the patient (i.e., through patient surveys) with an overall view on the patient experience, and in part, through process improvement, financial and operational data that indicate whether they are meeting their financial and quality outcome goals.

■ Payers have tended to measure quality based on costs and outcome measures–particularly process of care measures. They know that these types of measures are correlated with overall improved outcomes and reduced costs of care that ultimately improves their bottom line. Employers, who pay the premiums on health insurance benefits for their employees, perceive quality in the productivity of their workforce: Was the employee given the correct medical care in a timely way? Was the employee back at work and productive as soon as possible?

In short, there are varying views and definitions of quality across the spectrum of patients, professionals and organizations related to healthcare. However, increasingly, as payers design reimbursement structures to reward providers for improvements in specific quality metrics, providers intensify process improvement initiatives, and create structures such as the medical home and accountable care organizations, in order to ensure quality improvements in an environment in which they are paid for value not volume.

Measurement is essential to achieving quality improvement in any endeavor, particularly in healthcare. Again, a definition from CMS: "Quality measures are standards for measuring the performance of healthcare providers to care for patients and populations. Quality measures can identify important aspects of care like safety, effectiveness, timeliness, and fairness." (2) Quality measures are generally focused on broad areas of patient care such as outcomes, processes, safety, patient perceptions and others.

9.3 The Healthcare Quality Problem

The IOM's report, *To Err is Human: Building a Safer Health System*, not only reported the number of deaths from preventable medical errors but also called for a concerted focus on improving processes. It advised that, while adverse events may occur in the medical delivery setting, some of them may not be preventable, but many are. The approach to reducing the occurrence of medical errors is systemic. According to the Institute for Healthcare Improvement (IHI),

> good people simply working harder will be insufficient to overcome the complexities inherent in today's systems of care to prevent errors and harm to patients. Errors will occur, the key is to design the care delivery systems so that harm does not reach the patient.
>
> (3)

In *To Err is Human*, the Institute of Medicine noted that

> a major force for improving patient safety is the intrinsic motivation of health care providers . . . but the interaction between factors in the external environment and factors inside healthcare organizations can also prompt the changes needed to improve patient safety.
>
> (3)

External environmental factors include the availability of knowledge and tools to reduce errors and measure results, leadership, financing mechanisms, public policy initiatives, and the demands of patients and purchasers. Factors internal to the healthcare organization include leadership, a culture of learning from errors, and an effective patient safety program. In its report, the IOM laid out recommendations for addressing the problem based on a "four-tiered approach," including:

> establishing a national focus to create leadership, research, tools and protocols to enhance the knowledge about safety; identifying and learning from errors through immediate and strong mandatory reporting efforts (and creating an environment that encourages organizations to identify errors, evaluate causes, and take appropriate actions to improve future performance); raising the standards and expectations for improvements in safety through the actions of oversight organizations, group purchasers, and professional groups; creating safety systems inside healthcare organizations through the implementation of safe practices at the delivery level.
>
> (3)

One of the core issues of efforts to improve patient safety in hospitals is the provider's reluctance to report errors due to the threat of litigation. While the

IOM report acknowledges that events resulting in harm to the patient should not be kept from the public eye, the "legal discoverability of information may undercut motivations to detect and analyze errors." (3) The related data should be ensured protection so that errors will not continue to be hidden. Instead, reporting of errors provides the information to understand their root causes and to improve processes and organizational structures to prevent similar errors in the future. Some states have already enacted legislation to provide just this protection. One of them is Florida, where each healthcare facility is required to designate an appropriately trained person to inform each patient, or an individual identified under the provisions of the law, about when an adverse medical incident happens to them that results in serious harm to the patient. According to the law, that notification to the patient does not constitute an acknowledgment or admission of liability and may not be introduced as evidence in court (Fla. Stat. Title 29, § 395. 1051). (4) Other States, including Michigan, have also passed legislation that supports this type of information sharing and, as discussed in Chapter 7, the medical apology can be an effective approach to informing the patient of a medical error that has occurred in their care.

In 2001, subsequent to the issuance of the 1999 IOM report on safety, the IOM published a second report, *Crossing the Quality Chasm*, in which it laid out principles to guide healthcare providers in their quest to improve quality of care. *Crossing the Quality Chasm* focused on how the "health system can be reinvented to foster innovation and improve the delivery of care" (5) and presented a strategy and plan for the future. This report offered six aims for healthcare, suggesting that care delivery be:

- Safe
- Effective
- Patient-centered
- Timely
- Efficient
- Equitable

The report also offered ten rules for redesign of the care delivery system:

1. Care is based on continuous healing relationships–patients should receive care when they need it and in the form in which they need it.
2. Care is customized according to patient needs and values–common types of patient needs should be met, and the system should be responsive to patient needs and choices.

3. The patient is the source of control–patients should have the information they need and [be] given the opportunity to exercise as much control as they want to take.
4. Knowledge is shared and information flows freely–patients should have complete access to their medical information and communication between patients and clinicians should be effective.
5. Decision-making is evidence based–that is, reliant on the best available scientific knowledge.
6. Safety is a system priority.
7. Transparency is necessary–the system should make available to patients and their families the information they need to make informed choices.
8. Needs are anticipated–the system should not wait to react but should anticipate patient needs.
9. Waste is continuously decreased–resources and patient time should not be wasted.
10. Cooperation among clinicians is a priority–clinicians and provider organizations should collaborate and cooperate in patient care.

(5)

Finally, *Crossing the Quality Chasm* addressed the environment in which patient safety would be advanced. It identified four main areas in which change is needed: application of scientific evidence to decision-making; availability and use of information systems; alignment of payment policies with quality improvement; and preparing the workforce. (5)

9.4 Challenge of Quality and Safety in Healthcare Delivery

A number of factors make improvements in healthcare quality challenging. Healthcare is delivered locally, and as such, the delivery system has evolved with more than 5,000 hospitals that generally operate independently of one another, with over 16,000 nursing homes that operate similarly, and with ambulatory facilities, specialty hospitals, and clinicians also functioning generally without a central focus of control (i.e., control of quality using processes similar to those found, for instance, in air travel). Not only is healthcare a fragmented "system," it also has as its "product" the health of very complicated human bodies mended through the complex and sophisticated structures, science, human skills, and technologies of care delivery.

Further complicating improvement in patient safety across the country, is extensive geographic variation in the way in which healthcare is delivered. This variation is in the clinical procedures that are used, in the levels of clinical skills among practitioners, and in the array of evidence to support decision-making across the multiplicity of possible diagnoses and clinical interventions. Variation is found not only in care delivery but also in quality and in costs in various regions across the country. The *Dartmouth Atlas of Health Care* reported, based on 2018 data, that "Despite . . . aggregate improvements and changes over time in expenditures, readmission rates and quality of care continue to exhibit wide variation." (6) In other words, higher cost does not implicitly mean better quality. In many regions of the country, there is substantially more money spent on healthcare while quality in some of those regions is poorer than in other lower cost areas.

9.5 Standardization/Accreditation

A first step in reducing costly variation in cost and in improving quality may be through improved protocols of care i.e., standardization. Standardization among hospitals and in medical education has a long history. Standards for healthcare services have a variety of sources. They are developed and adopted by regulatory and semi-regulatory bodies such as government payers and accreditation agencies. They are imposed through licensure boards, and by professional membership organizations. They are also developed internally in individual provider organizations.

9.5.1 The Joint Commission

Although the American College of Surgeons initiated its work toward standardization in hospitals in 1913, it was not until 1951 that a hospital accrediting body was formally launched. The Joint Commission on Accreditation of Hospitals (JCAH) was founded through the collaboration of the American College of Surgeons, the American College of Physicians, the American Hospital Association, the American Medical Association, and the Canadian Medical Association. The JCAH began offering voluntary accreditation to hospitals in 1953. A few years later, the Canadian Medical Association withdrew from the JCAH and later, in 1979, the American Dental Association joined as a corporate member.

Twelve years after the founding of the JCAH, when the Social Security Amendments of 1965 were passed into law, Congress provided that hospitals accredited by JCAH would be "deemed" to be in compliance with most of the Medicare Conditions of Participation for Hospitals and thus able to participate in the Medicare and Medicaid programs for reimbursement of services. This was a key incentive that drove hospitals to seek accreditation. In 1988, JCAH changed its name to the Joint Commission on Accreditation of Healthcare Organizations (JCAHO) to "reflect the expanded scope of activities" (7) that included accreditation of hospice programs, and long-term care, ambulatory care, home care, managed care, and behavioral healthcare programs. Program expansions in subsequent years included accreditation and certification services for clinical laboratories, critical access hospitals, and a wider spectrum of disease-specific care programs. This brought about a further name change in 2007 to The Joint Commission. (7)

The Joint Commission evaluates and accredits more than 22,000 healthcare organizations and programs in the United States and provides accreditation globally in other countries under the organizational structure of Joint Commission International. It functions as an independent, not-for-profit organization. To earn and maintain accreditation and receive the Joint Commission's Gold Seal of Approval™, an organization must undergo an on-site survey by a survey team at least every three years.

In its governance structure, a 21-member Board of Commissioners includes representatives from each of the Joint Commission's corporate members as well as seven at-large members. The President and Chief Executive Officer is an ex-officio member of the board. In addition to the types of organizations accredited by the Joint Commission (listed in Table 9.1), certifications are given to qualifying health programs and services.

9.5.2 DNV Healthcare, Inc.

DNV is a hospital accrediting organization based in Houston, Texas. Its parent organization is Det Norske Ventas (DNV), a nongovernmental foundation based in Oslo, Norway. DNV bases its approach to hospital accreditation on International Organization for Standardization (IOS) standards and principles. DNV was given "deemed" status by the Centers for Medicare and Medicaid Services (CMS) in 2008, which means that its accreditation of healthcare organizations meets the criteria for Medicare conditions of participation. Almost 500 U.S. hospitals are DNV accredited. (8) DNV's outcomes-based approach to accreditation is one in which its professional accreditors

Table 9.1   The Joint Commission's Accreditation and Certification Services

■ General, psychiatric, children's and rehabilitation hospitals
■ Critical access hospitals
■ Medical equipment services, hospice services, and other home care organizations
■ Nursing homes and other long-term care facilities
■ Behavioral healthcare organizations and addiction services
■ Rehabilitation centers, group practices, office-based surgeries, and other ambulatory care providers
■ Independent or freestanding laboratories
■ Assisted living communities
■ Pharmacy

Source: The Joint Commission. Accreditation and Certification. Available at www.joint-commission.org/

are actively engaged with its accredited hospitals on an ongoing basis to help them identify and correct unsafe practices and to engage in continuous quality improvement.

9.5.3 *The National Committee for Quality Assurance*

The National Committee for Quality Assurance (NCQA) is an accrediting body for managed care organizations. The rapid expansion of managed care in the late 1980s and the rapidly growing interest of major employers in managed care generated an interest in a method of reviewing and reporting the level of quality with which managed care organizations operated and in formally accrediting them relative to quality standards. In the late 1980s, the managed care industry was expanding dramatically. Within a few years, there were hundreds of managed care plans in the U.S., and with their expansion, the levels of quality among them varied dramatically. A structure was needed to reduce that variability and to ensure that they met quality standards. In light of this growth, the Robert Wood Johnson Foundation provided grant funding to an industry trade group to assess the feasibility of creating an accrediting program that would review and evaluate managed care programs based on quality indicators. (9)

Emerging from that study in 1990, the National Committee for Quality Assurance (NCQA) was formed as a private, 501(c)(3) not-for-profit organization. The formation of NCQA was influenced by the input of employers, unions, health plans and consumers. Its role is to improve healthcare quality for the 191 million people who are enrolled in managed care organizations through their health insurance plans.

Developed with the input and support of employers, unions, health plans, and consumers, the NCQA sets its standards with a view to encourage health plans to continuously enhance quality. NCQA health plan accreditation is designed to help employers and consumers distinguish and make choices among health plans based on quality. Health plan accreditation evaluates not only the core systems and processes that make up a health plan but also the actual results that the plan achieves on key dimensions of care and service.

The NCQA review process consists of onsite and offsite evaluations conducted by survey teams of physicians and managed care experts. The Review Oversight Committee, a national oversight committee of physicians, analyzes the teams' findings and assigns an accreditation status based on a plan's compliance with NCQA standards and its performance, relative to other plans, on selected Healthcare Effectiveness Data and Information Set (HEDIS). Performance measures, such as immunization and mammography rates and member satisfaction are the focus of the survey tool. HEDIS is used by more than 90 percent of health plans to measure performance on important dimensions of care and service.

9.6 Quality Improvement Initiatives

Quality improvement has not only been the focus of accrediting bodies. It is the mission of efforts by individual hospitals, governmental initiatives, and other organizations and initiatives. A short discussion of some of these follows.

9.6.1 National Quality Organizations and Agencies

9.6.1.1 The National Quality Forum

In 1998, the President's Advisory Commission on Consumer Protection and Quality in the Healthcare Industry recommended the creation of a national forum in which all of healthcare's stakeholders could come together to find ways to improve the quality and safety of healthcare in the United States. This recommendation led to the 1999 creation of the National Quality Forum (NQF), a private, not-for-profit, public benefit corporation. NQF is a consensus-based organization that was created through the work of a coalition of private and public sector leaders whose goal is to "promote and ensure patient protections and healthcare quality through measurement and public reporting." (10) The NQF has endorsed more than 300 quality measures, including performance measures, quality indicators, preferred practices, and reporting guidelines. These are used in over 20 federal public reporting and pay-for-performance programs along with public and private sector programs. DHHS uses guidance from NQF to "foster the use of a more uniform set of measures across federal programs that provide health coverage for about 120 million Americans" e.g., Medicare. (10)

9.6.1.2 Centers for Medicare and Medicaid Services

CMS is the largest single payer of health services in the country, and, as such, has a particular interest in ensuring that the care rendered to its enrollees produces quality outcomes. CMS is using reimbursement incentive programs to accomplish this. For example, a provision of the PPACA calls for the development of Accountable Care Organizations who assume responsibility for the health of a defined population and are incentivized to work with those populations to improve their health status and reduce their demand for medical care, i.e., to improve the quality of the care they deliver and the outcomes of that care.

The CMS has also launched other initiatives to assure quality in the care provided to Medicare beneficiaries.

∎ **Quality Improvement Organizations (QIOs)**

The QIO Program is a major federal initiative to improve healthcare quality for Medicare enrollees. Quality improvement organizations (QIOs) are established under the requirements of Sections 1152–1154 of the Social Security Act and are comprised of healthcare quality experts, clinicians, and consumers. Their objective is broad: to improve the quality of care delivered to Medicare enrollees. QIOs in each state and the District of Columbia, Puerto Rico, and the U.S. Virgin Islands, under CMS administration, are designated to work at a local level to improve patient care in the healthcare delivery entities in the area and to improve and integrate care for the local populations and communities. QIOs are private, mostly not-for-profit organizations, staffed primarily by doctors and other clinical healthcare professionals. They perform peer review of the medical care that is provided in the locality and communities that they serve and work collaboratively with providers to improve healthcare quality. (11)

■ Premier Hospital Quality Incentive Demonstration (PHQID)

One of CMS's quality initiatives to assess the relationship between financial incentives and quality improvement was the Premier Hospital Quality Incentive Demonstration or PHQID that ran from 2003 to 2009. This demonstration was designed to assess whether or not financial incentive programs are effective in achieving measurable quality improvement in inpatient care in five clinical areas. In practice, the demonstration sought to improve the quality of inpatient care for Medicare beneficiaries by giving financial incentives (bonuses) to almost 300 hospitals for measurable quality performance on designated quality indicators related to the five clinical areas. The PHQID project was essentially designed to determine if economic incentives provided to hospitals are effective at improving the quality of inpatient care. Public reporting on the demonstration project indicated that "over the course of the demonstration approximately 10 percent of all participating hospitals moved from the bottom to the top 20 percent in one or more clinical areas, improving quality scores by an average 29.2 percentage points." (12)

■ Hospital Compare Public Reporting of Performance Measures

CMS maintains a consumer-oriented website that provides information on how well specific hospitals provide recommended care to their patients. On this site, the consumer can see the recommended care that an adult should get if being treated for a variety of conditions such as heart attack, heart failure, or pneumonia or if having surgery. The site can be accessed at www.medicare.gov/hospitalcompare. Consumers and other interested persons can find performance and cost data on the hospital(s) of their choice and are able to see data on how those hospitals compare with national averages and with other hospitals in a given region.

9.6.1.3 Institute for Healthcare Improvement

The Institute for Healthcare Improvement (IHI) is an independent not-for-profit organization founded by Donald Berwick, MD, in 1991 and based in Cambridge, MA. IHI positions itself to "bring awareness of safety and quality to millions, accelerate learning and the systemic improvement of care, develop solutions to previously intractable challenges, and mobilize health systems, communities, regions, and nations to reduce harm and deaths." (13)

IHI's mission emphasizes an approach to healthcare quality improvement that includes:

- The use of scientific evidence
- Putting the patient and family at the center of the process of improvement
- A focus on patient safety
- Reducing the cost of care

A major project of IHI in the U.S., is the "Triple Aim" whose framework identifies three focus areas that must be simultaneously addressed in order to achieve systemic quality improvement. These three focus areas are improving population health, enhancing the patient experience and outcomes of care, and reducing the per capita cost of care. The Triple Aim has served as a foundational approach in initiatives to improve healthcare during COVID-19.

While IHI continues its work in the U.S., it has also established itself as a global force for change with operations in countries such as Brazil where it has worked with the Brazilian Ministry of Health, the National Regulatory Agency and local leading healthcare providers to lower the rate of cesarean sections which were the highest in the world. By 2018, they had together significantly increased the number of vaginal births from 21.6 percent to 38 percent of all births. With funding from the Bill and Melinda Gates Foundation, IHI opened an office in Addis Ababa to collaborate with the Ethiopian Ministry of Health to transform the national healthcare system and particularly to reduce the number of maternal and neonatal deaths. IHI is engaged in other similar projects around the world. (13)

9.7 Evidence-Based Medicine

In the 1990s, evidence-based medicine (EBM) emerged as a way to improve and evaluate patient care for the individual and to establish guidelines or standards of care. In EBM, research evidence is used in conjunction with the patient's values to make decisions about the best medical care for the patient. Using EBM, individual clinical expertise is integrated with the best external evidence from research and practice. "It is the conscientious, explicit, and judicious use of current best evidence in making decisions about the care of individual patients." (14)

What clinicians know about illnesses, diseases, injuries, and their effective treatment is expanding continuously. However, the health professional of today cannot keep pace with the rapidly growing body of knowledge that is generated by research and the researcher's analysis of the enormous amount of data that is made available through the implementation of information systems that support real-time collection of data from the clinical and business sectors of healthcare. In using EBM, clinicians access the best current published research literature and apply their expertise and experience, to provide the patient with the best advice and judgment possible in state-of-the-art medicine. Additionally, practice guidelines and clinical protocols are established using best evidence and research to further help clinicians and their patients make the best decisions regarding clinical care.

9.8 Never Events

"Never events" are, quite literally, those events that should never occur in the delivery of medical care. They are simply preventable errors. According to the CMS, "'Never events,' like surgery on the wrong body part or a mismatched blood transfusion, cause serious injury or death to beneficiaries, and result in increased cost to the Medicare Program to treat the consequences of the error." (15) The medical services to correct the error and care for any adverse outcomes can cost tens of thousands of dollars or more, and cause pain and suffering, or worse, death, for the patient. Historically, hospitals and physicians involved in performing a procedure in which a never event occurred have been reimbursed the cost of correcting that error (if that error did not result in death, of course). After studying these types of events for several years, CMS announced in 2008 that it would no longer pay the costs of never events–hospitals and doctors would be compelled to correct the error, provide all needed services to the patient to correct the resulting problem, and do so at their own cost.

After the CMS adopted the policy of no longer paying the costs of medical care to remedy never events, it also encouraged state Medicaid programs to follow suit. Many have done so, as have private insurance companies. Hospitals and physicians are being denied reimbursement for the costs of fixing a condition that should not have occurred. This negative financial incentive, along with any civil action, impacts hospitals' and other providers' commitment to increase the pace of process improvement in order to reduce the number of never events that occur in their institutions and offices.

Hospitals and doctors are vigilant about implementing processes that improve patient safety and prevent never events. For example, in surgical cases, the surgeon will see the patient before surgery to confirm in detail the name of the patient, the procedure that will be done, and the site on the patient on which the surgery is to be performed. This includes the patient or doctor placing a mark on the site of the patient's body on which the surgery will be performed. In addition, before surgery begins, a "timeout" is typically called in order for all personnel in the room to confirm who the patient is, what procedure is to be done, and the area of the patient's body on which to perform surgery. Many providers have also adopted the process improvement principle in which any member of the team can call a timeout during surgery should he or she observe anything questionable.

Since the never-event policy was adopted, the list of never events has been modified a number of times. Today, that list has 29 "serious reportable events" grouped into seven categories:

■ Surgical or procedural events
■ Product or device events
■ Patient protection events
■ Care management events
■ Environmental events
■ Radiologic events
■ Criminal events

(16)

9.9 The Patient-Centered Medical Home

Chronic conditions afflict at least 45 percent of the U.S. population, and more than 80 percent of Medicare enrollees have at least one chronic condition. When there is a lack of coordination of care of these individuals and management of their conditions, costs escalate. Duplicative diagnostic tests are often ordered by different providers, patients return home from a hospitalization without clear understanding of medication protocols, often to be readmitted within a short period, others receive medications that interfere with one another, and overall their care is not appropriately managed. The concept of the patient-centered medical home was developed to address these issues. The medical home is not necessarily a place: it is a team of primary care providers (doctor, nurse, other clinicians) whose role it is to coordinate the care of the patient. The typical model of a PCMH is that of a care manager functioning within a physician's primary care practice as part of the care team. The team provides primary care services, but beyond that, the care manager also (1) arranges specialist care, (2) follows up with patients to ensure that they are compliant with diet and exercise plans and that they understand which medications they are prescribed and how and when to take them, and (3) overall, manages the care of the patient in order to prevent the onset of acute episodes of one or more of the chronic conditions that the patient has. Initial studies of the effectiveness of medical homes indicate that they can significantly reduce costs, decrease hospital re-admissions and emergency room visits and can support the patient in living a more productive and healthy life.

9.10 Tools for Quality Improvement

9.10.1 Dashboards

A quality dashboard is a graphic array of information that highlights an organization's performance in a number of designated areas of quality. It is meant to be visual, with data contained in a small amount of space.

The dashboard should include [at least one] variable from each of the following nine topic areas: outcomes frequently compared with nationally established benchmarks; critical national initiatives; publicly reported data; progress on local initiatives; patient satisfaction; patient complaints and potential lawsuits; significant incidents; workforce issues, such as retention; and peer review summaries. Specifics will vary by hospital and service area, but when all variables are put together, a comprehensive picture will emerge of the quality of care being delivered and of improvement toward established benchmarks. (17)

9.10.2 Measures and Benchmarks

Benchmarking is the process of establishing a standard of excellence and comparing a business function or activity, a product, or an enterprise as a whole with that standard. As a component of total quality management, benchmarking is a continuous process by which an organization can measure and compare its own processes with those of organizations that are leaders in a particular area. (18)

Benchmarking must be a team process because the outcome will involve changing current practices. This will impact the entire organization. The team should represent a cross-section of the organization and include members who have subject knowledge; communications and computer proficiency; skills as facilitators and outside contacts; and, very important, the sponsorship of senior management. Benchmarking requires quantitative measurement of the subject. The types of measurements used will depend on the process or activity that is being benchmarked. Typically, "benchmarking metrics can be classified in one of four categories: productivity, quality, time and cost-related." (18)

9.11 Summary

Quality process improvement is one of the most demanding and important areas of work in healthcare management. Following the 1999 release of the IOM report *To Err is Human*, healthcare providers, payers, and consumers faced the reality tens of thousands of patients dying and many more suffering adverse events due to preventable medical errors. In the decades since the release of the IOM report, new initiatives and incentive programs have been launched in every sector of healthcare to improve patient safety, reduce errors, and restore a sense of confidence in medical delivery. The medical errors that occur are primarily generated not through the negligence of caregivers but through the lack of processes that can be put in place to reduce errors. Hospitals are now required to publicly report their outcomes on key indicators that indicate their accuracy in following correct protocols for care. Hospitals are ranked against one another for these indicators, and as the public becomes more aware of and accesses these rankings, it is believed they will make more informed choices about their care providers. This is only one of many steps that address the issue of quality improvement in healthcare–there are many others as discussed in this chapter. Additionally, information systems and the use of process improvement methods, such as Six Sigma, as well as payer incentives for quality improvement and disincentives related to never events, are all initiatives that hover over and drive improvement.

References

1. CMS. *Quality measurement and improvement.* Available at www.cms. gov/Medicare/Quality-Initiatives-Patient-Assessment-Instruments/MMS/ Quality-Measure-and-Quality-Improvement-.

2. 2: CMS. *What is a quality measure?* Available at www.cms.gov/Medicare/Quality-Initiatives-Patient-Assessment-Instruments/MMS/NTM-What-is-a-Quality-Measure-SubPage.

3. Institute of Medicine. 1999. *To err is human: Building a safer health system.* Executive Summary. Washington, DC: National Academies Press, pp. 4 and 6. Available at www.ncbi.nlm.nih.gov/books/NBK225179/.

4. The 2020 Florida Statutes. *Title XX1X, Chapter 395.* Available at www.leg.state.fl.us/statutes/index.cfm?App_mode=Display_Statute&URL=0300-0399/0395/Sections/0395.1051.html#:~:text=395.1051%20Duty%20to%20notify%20patients.%E2%80%94%20An%20appropriately%20trained,that%20result%20in%20serious%20harm%20to%20the%20patient.

5. Institute of Medicine. 2002. *Crossing the quality chasm: A new health system for the 21st century.* Washington, DC: National Academies Press. Available at https://pubmed.ncbi.nlm.nih.gov/25057539/.

6. K. Bronner, ED. 2021 (Aug. 18). The Dartmouth atlas of healthcare: 2018 data update. *The Dartmouth Institute for Health Policy and Clinical Practice.* Available at https://data.dartmouthatlas.org/downloads/reports/2018_data_report_081821.pdf.

7. The Joint Commission 70-year tiimeline. Available at www.jointcommission.org/-/media/enterprise-imagery/70th-anniversary/tjc-70-year-timeline-81121.pdf.

8. DNV GL Healthcare. 2008 (Sept. 26). *Medicare approves DNV to accredit hospitals.* Available at www.dnvglhealthcare.com/releases/test-medicare-approves-dnv-to-accredithospitals#:~:text=Medicare%20Approves%20DNV%20to%20Accredit%20Hospitals%20HOUSTON%2C%20Sept.,hospital%20accreditation%20organization%20in%20more%20than%2030%20years.

9. S.L. Isaacs and D.C. Colby (eds.). 2008. *The Robert Wood Johnson anthology to improve health and health care.* Vol. 11. San Francisco: Jossey-Bass, p. 11.

10. National Quality Forum. *NQF's work in quality measurement.* Available at www.qualityforum.org/about_nqf/work_in_quality_measurement/.

11. CMS.gov. *Quality improvement organizations.* Available at ttps://www.cms.gov/Medicare/Quality-Initiatives-Patient-Assessment-Instruments/QualityImprovement Orgs/Downloads/CMS-QIO-Current-Work-Archive-Fact-Sheet-QIO-Overview.pdf. Updated February 11, 2020.

12. R. Bankowitz. 2012 (May 2). The hospital quality incentive demonstration program: A record of success. *Health Affairs Blog.* Available at www.healthaffairs.org/do/10.1377/hblog20120502.019023/full/.

13. Institute for Healthcare Improvement. *About IHI.* Available at www.ihi.org/about/Pages/default.aspx.

14. A.D. Oxman, D.L. Sackett, G.H. Guyatt, and the Evidence-Based Medicine Working Group. 1993. *Users guide to evidence-based medicine.* Vol. 270, No. 17. Chicago: American Medical Association, pp. 2093–2095.

15. CMS. 2006 (May 18). *Eliminating serious, preventable, and costly medical errors: Never events.* Available at www.cms.gov/newsroom/fact-sheets/eliminating-serious-preventable-and-costly-medical-errors-never-events#:~:text=According%

20to%20the%20National%20Quality%20Forum%20%28NQF%29%2C%20
%E2%80%9Cnever,for%20%E2%80%9Cnever%20events%E2%80%9D%20are%20
listed%20in%20Appendix%201.
16. Agency for Healthcare Research and Quality. 2019 (Sept. 7). *Never events.*
Available at https://psnet.ahrq.gov/primer/never-events.
17. L. Larson. 2008 (May). How to drive a quality dashboard. Interview with Eric
D. Lister, MD, managing director of Ki Associates, Portsmouth, NY. H&HN.
18. H.R. Benson. 1994. An introduction of Benchmarking. *Radiology Management,*
16(3): 35–392.

Chapter 10

Public Health

10.1 Introduction

The CDC Foundation defines public health as

> the science of protecting and improving the health of people and
> their communities. This work is achieved by promoting healthy
> lifestyles, researching disease and injury prevention, and detect-
> ing, preventing and responding to infectious diseases. Overall,
> public health is concerned with protecting the health of entire
> populations.
>
> (1)

At the federal level, the Centers for Disease Control and Prevention (CDC) is
the nation's preeminent public health agency.

Public health in the United States is the "other arm" of healthcare delivery. Public health is primarily focused on the health of the population, on
collection and analysis of data on disease and injury patterns and their
causes, and on developing and implementing policies and practices that
address population health problems. Their core goal is to improve the health
status of the population.

Public health services are provided through governmental support at the
local community, state, and federal levels. The core roles of public health
service are assessment, policy development and quality assurance. At a local
level, public health services provide primary and preventive services, such
as vaccine inoculations. These services generally serve the needs of persons

who otherwise lack access to basic and preventive medical care and they serve the needs of the broader population when faced with infectious diseases such as occurred during the COVID-19 pandemic.

Public health is oriented toward the health of the populations, looking broadly at the conditions and incidences of disease or injury that occur within the population and providing services (e.g., immunizations) and information to control the spread of disease. While the public health sector is a critical part of the infrastructure of providing medical care in the United States, it is not generally tied into the private medical sector providers of care. Public health is distinct from the providers and payers that serve the acute care needs of the population of the United States.

Public health services are provided not only through government agencies, but also through a plethora of voluntary organizations in communities across the country such as the Red Cross and faith-based and civic-minded groups who have a goal of improving access to healthcare services for underserved populations. Services and facilities owned by these groups can be found in metropolitan and rural locations and include, for example, shelters where health screening and basic assistance may be provided. While these are important organizations in the overall support and improvement of the public's health in the United States, they are not structurally tied to the public health system.

Public health services are offered at all levels of government: federal, state, and local. While there are responsibilities that are similar at each level (e.g., gathering and reporting of vital health data), each has duties that reflect the level of government at which they are organized. For example, the local health department may be involved in operating primary care clinics, while at the state and federal levels, a corollary responsibility is to provide health services after a major disaster, e.g., post-Katrina or during a pandemic. Coordination between and among the various levels of public health agencies is critical to their functioning. That coordination primarily revolves around the development of guidance from the CDC to the States and local agencies and the reporting of data from the local level, up to the States and to the CDC. Putting this in the global context, the CDC and its corollary agencies in other countries report disease indicators and other health status data to the World Health Organization (WHO) to monitors globally for infectious disease outbreaks and for coordination of services after a disaster.

A 2012 IOM, report *Primary Care and Public Health: Exploring Integration to Improve Population Health,* called on the CDC and the Health Resources and Services Administration (HRSA) to examine the integration of public health and private primary care organizations in order to better achieve national population health objectives. (2) Under the PPACA, both the CDC and HRSA are authorized to initiate new population health programs. It also authorized funding incentives for private providers to develop medical homes and Accountable Care Organizations (ACOs), both of which focus on primary care and prevention. The IOM, in its report, encourages both sectors of healthcare, private and public, to collaborate in the interests of improving the health of local communities through care coordination, data sharing, and integration of services. (2) In short, there is an increasing recognition of the intersection between the work of public health and private healthcare delivery providers.

This chapter will focus on the work of designated government agencies that are involved in research, data collection and dissemination, disaster relief and the provision of primary medical services in medically underserved areas and for those who lack access to basic care.

10.2 Role of Public Health

The IOM defines the role of public health as "what we, as a society, do collectively to assure the conditions for people to be healthy." (3) In its early days, the work of public health agencies was focused primarily on the physical health of the population, but by the turn of the twenty-first century, that role took on a more comprehensive and holistic mission. In 1994, a collaborative of stakeholders from all sectors of public health and levels of government undertook an effort to assist national, state, and local public health agencies define and focus on public health goals. In this effort, they collaboratively defined the vision of public health as "Healthy People in Healthy Communities," a vision that suggests that all factors that impact a population's health should be considered cohesively in order to improve health status. The six public health responsibilities that were identified to fulfill this vision are to:

1. Prevent epidemics and spread of disease
2. Protect against environmental hazards
3. Prevent injuries
4. Promote and encourage healthy behavior
5. Respond to disasters and assist communities in recovery
6. Assure the quality and accessibility of health services

These responsibilities apply to all levels of public health–federal, state, county, city, and community. Each has a part in assuring, for example, that citizens are protected against environmental hazards. For instance, the local public health department has authority to act when a public building contains suspect or potentially harmful materials, to ban smoking in public places in order to prevent harm to the public from second-hand smoke, and to provide public health clinics and/or educational programs to assure that otherwise under-served populations have access to certain basic services. At the state level, these responsibilities are carried out through activities such as licensure of professionals to assure the appropriate professional preparation of healthcare practitioners, provision of mental health hospitals to assure accessibility to services that would otherwise be unavailable to persons without the financial means to pay for those services, and the funding of educational programs.

Likewise, the federal government holds responsibility in each of the six public health functions identified in the Healthy People, Healthy Communities initiative. For example, the Centers for Disease Control and Prevention (CDC) gathers data for assessment of epidemics and takes measures to prevent outbreaks of disease and helps to provide reporting and services in times of disaster and the Food and Drug Administration (FDA) is responsible for the safety of the food supply and of drugs.

While there are agencies at each level of government (federal, state, and local) that have defined responsibilities in public health, each has interconnected roles. For example, health data are gathered on an ongoing basis–the local government collects vital statistics and reports those to the state level from which, in turn, they are reported to the federal government (the CDC). On the global stage, the World Health Organization holds leadership, oversight, and administrative responsibility in these six areas for all its member countries. It is important to understand that from the local to the global level, public health responsibilities are interrelated through reporting mechanisms and through programs of education and planning/implementation of health services that relate to detecting illness and to improving and maintaining the health of populations.

10.3 A Brief History of the Public Health Service

As discussed briefly in Chapter 1, the origins of public health are found in centuries of evolving health services and the government's assumption of responsibility for the protection of the health of the population. In the formative days of the country, the United States shared a common interest with countries in Europe where commercial interests and the viability and vibrancy of towns and cities were reliant upon a healthy population—one that could be productive and could contribute to the economic growth of the municipality and the country. With the growth of crowded cities along the East Coast of the United States, the vulnerability of the population to disease was endemic. Sanitary conditions were challenging, and the lack of public services to address health issues was a concern to government and to business.

As cities took on responsibility to assure the sanitary conditions of the city and to provide medical care to their indigent residents who otherwise would not have access to care, the numbers of clinics and almshouses where physicians could work grew. However, along the coastal cities, many people working on ships were not residents of the country and thus were not the responsibility of the city. To prevent diseases from entering the country via merchant ships, to provide services to treat the illnesses and injuries that seamen experienced, and to support the vitality of the maritime trades, the federal government implemented the Marine Hospital Service in 1798. Under the Marine Hospital Service, hospitals and clinics were developed in major coastal cities and ports. First among these was the Marine Hospital set up in Boston Harbor. As this initiative evolved over the next century, the Marine Hospital Service became the U.S. Public Health Service in 1912 and took on responsibilities that reached well beyond seamen to include the urban and rural populations across the country.

It was not until the mid-nineteenth century that local governments also began to formally take on responsibility for the health of their communities. In the middle of the nineteenth century, the 1850 Report of the Sanitary Commission of Massachusetts prepared by Lemuel Shattuck, a statistician, documented the results of unsanitary and environmental conditions, and found that death and disease were related to the level of unsanitary conditions in which people lived in cities. (5) This report recommended that cities establish structures such as Boards of Health to gather vital statistics and perform research on public health conditions, address the health of school children and the training of nurses, and oversee and have authority over infrastructure (e.g., housing and slums, products and processes that impacted the environment, disposal of waste, location of cemeteries, etc.). However, it was not until almost a decade and a half later that New York decided to investigate the living environments in the city and to gather vital statistics in order to determine morbidity and mortality rates (illness and deaths) of populations in the city.

The study reported such egregious unsanitary conditions in the city's housing that the first local Board of Health was created in New York and given the authority and the resources to address the unsanitary conditions in the city's slums. This Board of Health signaled a turning point for public health in the United States as cities took on responsibility to assure the sanitary conditions of the city and to provide medical care to their indigent residents who otherwise would not have access to care. Clinics and almshouses, where physicians worked, grew as cities took on this responsibility.

10.4 The U.S. Public Health Service Today

At the federal level, public health services are organized within the executive branch of the government, under the auspices and direction of the Department of Health and Human Services (HHS). The office of the Secretary of HHS has overall responsibility for the wide range of federal public health services that is available in the United States. HHS works closely with state and local governments, and many HHS-funded services are provided at the local level by state or county public health agencies and clinics or through private sector grantees.

HHS has multiple staff divisions and 11 operating divisions (shown in gray in Figure 10.1) that serve specific public health functions. Eight of these serve as the United States Public Health Service and three are designated as human services agencies. The eight departments within the Public Health Service are organized with the following functions:

1. The Agency for Healthcare Research and Quality (AHRQ) whose role is to "produce evidence to make healthcare safer, higher quality, more accessible, equitable, and affordable, and to work within the U.S. Department of Health and Human Services and with other partners to make sure that the evidence is understood and used." (6)
2. The Agency for Toxic Substances and Disease Registry (ATSDR) "protects communities from harmful health effects related to exposure to natural and man-made hazardous substances." The agency performs services such as responding to environmental health emergencies, investigating emerging environmental health threats, conducting research on the health impacts of hazardous waste sites, etc. (7)
3. The Centers for Disease Control and Prevention (CDC) has been in the forefront of guiding public policy throughout the COVID-19 pandemic. Its role is to promote health and quality of life by preventing and controlling

disease, injury, and disability. The CDC works directly with public health functions at the state and local level in carrying out its functions and in implementing its guidance and policy recommendations. (8)

4. The Food and Drug Administration (FDA) has also been at the forefront of the COVID-19 pandemic as it provides emergency use authorization and ultimately final approval for the use of newly developed vaccines. Its role is to protect the public health by "ensuring the safety, efficacy, and security of human and veterinary drugs, biological products, and medical devices, and by ensuring the safety and security of the nations' food supply, cosmetics, and products that emit radiation." (9)

5. The Health Research and Services Administration (HRSA) serves a mission to "improve health outcomes and achieve health equity through access to quality services, a skilled health workforce, and innovative, high-value programs." The programs offered by HRSA "provide equitable healthcare to people who are geographically isolated and economically or medically vulnerable." (10)

6. The Indian Health Service (IHS) is focused on raising "the physical, mental, social, and spiritual health of American Indians and Alaska Natives to the highest level." (11)

7. The National Institutes of Health's (NIH) mission is "to seek fundamental knowledge about the nature and behavior of living systems and the application of that knowledge to enhance health, lengthen life, and reduce illness and disability." (12)

8. The Substance Abuse and Mental Health Services Administration's (SAMHSA's) mission is one of "reducing the impact of substance abuse and mental illness on America's communities." This agency was established by Congress in "1992 to make substance use and mental disorder information, services and research more accessible." (13)

The three human service agencies in the Department of Health and Human Services include:

1. The Center for Medicare and Medicaid Services (CMS) which administers Medicare and funding/regulation of Medicaid programs.

2. The Administration for Children and Families (ACF) to promote "the economic and social well-being of families, children, individuals, and communities with funding strategic partnerships, guidance, training and technical assistance." (14)

3. Administration for Community Living (ACL) was established in 2012 and brought together the prior Administration on Aging, Office on Disability,

and Administration on Developmental Disabilities. Its creation was based on the premise that persons with functional limitations of any type, including those related to aging, have a common interest in having access to home and community-based services. The ACL's objective is comprehensively to help "older adults and people with disabilities of all ages to live where and with whom they choose and fully participate in their communities. (15)

 – Also, a major office within the Public Health Service is the Office of the Surgeon General who serves as the country's chief health educator. The office is charged with providing the best scientific information available on how to improve health and decrease risk related to illness and injury. The Surgeon General is also the Vice Admiral of the U.S. Public Health Service Commissioned Corps who are assigned throughout the federal government in their mission to advance and protect the health of the population.

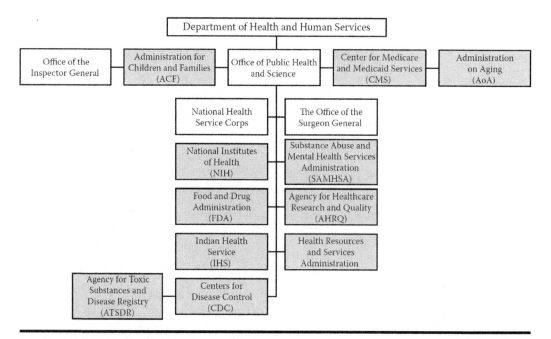

Figure 10.1 Organization Structure of the U.S. Office of Public Health and Science
Note: The operating divisions are in gray.
Source: From http:// hhs.gov/about/orgchart/

– The Office of the Surgeon General oversees the operations of the 6,000-member Commissioned Corps of the U.S. Public Health Service which is a major part of the U.S. Public Health Service. The Commissioned Corps was established in the late 1700s to protect the health of sailors and immigrants. Today, under the direction of the Surgeon General, "the U.S. Public Health Service Commissioned Corps is an elite team of more than 6,000 full-time, well-trained, highly qualified public health professionals dedicated to delivering the Nation's public health promotion and disease prevention programs and advancing public health science." (4) They serve in agencies throughout the federal government as doctors, dentists, nurses, veterinarians, engineers, scientists, and other health professionals.

– The Surgeon General is nominated by the President of the United States and confirmed by the U.S. Senate for a four-year term.

10.5 Healthy People 2030

In 1979 the Surgeon General issued his report, *Healthy People*, and with it laid the foundation for a national prevention agenda for improving the U.S. population health status. At the beginning of each decade since 1980, a broad-based consultation process has brought scientific knowledge to the development of national health objectives that could, and have, served as the basis for the development of state and community health prevention and intervention plans and have helped identify the measures for success in the implementation of those plans. The "Healthy People" initiative establishes overall objectives for the nation relative to top priority health concerns that have been enunciated through the process of consultation with leading scientists, healthcare, and community leaders and professionals from both the public and private sectors. The achievement of these objectives is monitored as an ongoing function and toward the end of each decade they are reassessed and modified to establish the plans for the next decade. In the 2020 adoption of the Healthy People plan, the leading health indicators reflect the major health concerns in the United States that are the focus of Healthy People 2030. Indicators were selected based on their importance as current public health issues and on the basis of their ability to motivate implementation action and establish data gathering processes to measure progress. The 2030 leading health indicators for persons of all ages include:

- Drug overdose deaths
- Exposure to unhealthy air
- Homicides
- Household insecurity and hunger
- Persons who are vaccinated annually against seasonal influenza
- Persons who know their HIV status
- Persons under the age of 65 with medical insurance
- Suicides
- Consumption of calories from added sugars by persons aged 2 years and over
- Use of the oral health system

(16)

The Healthy People program and reports have helped guide the proactive public health initiatives of states, counties, and municipalities across the country. Through a process of ongoing prioritization and program implementation, each of these levels of government has been able to bring about improved health status for the groups on which they have focused resources for health improvement. From their ongoing programs, they report before and after data relative to the level of achievement they have accomplished for their particular geographic area and targeted population(s).

10.6 2019 Novel Coronavirus Pandemic (COVID-19)

By definition, a pandemic is an "outbreak of a disease that occurs over a wide geographic area (such as multiple countries or continents) and typically affecting a significant proportion of the population." (17) "Epidemics" are outbreaks of disease that occurs in a defined geographic region. In short, a pandemic is global, an epidemic is a regional infectious disease spread. There have been pandemics previously in global history ever since humankind transitioned from being hunter-gatherers to an agrarian society. The Black Death in the fourteenth century killed an estimated 200 million people; The Russian flu of 1889–1893 spanned the globe in only four months and reappeared for three successive years killing over I million people; the Spanish flu spread silently around the globe before it was identified and it ultimately took approximately 50 million lives in 1918–1919. These are only a few of the pandemics that have taken a dramatic toll on human lives over the last several centuries. COVID-19 is the pandemic of the early twenty-first century.

The SARS-CoV-2, or COVID-19 pandemic was officially recognized in January of 2020 and is recorded to have taken over five million lives worldwide in less than two years. It is estimated that this number is lower than the actual numbers of persons who have succumbed to COVID-19 because of lack of recording and/or reporting of COVID-19-related deaths in some countries. In the U.S. alone, over 47 million COVID-19 cases and over 770,000 COVID-19 deaths were reported in the first two years of the pandemic. A hallmark of the COVID-19 pandemic is the widespread resistance to vaccination in many developed countries and lack of access to vaccines in underdeveloped countries. Without widespread vaccination, the virus had the opportunity to mutate and had done so repeatedly during its first years driving new surges in cases and deaths and the consequent surges in the need for hospital care to the point of overwhelming many hospitals and their staffs.

In the U.S., the pandemic highlighted the relationship between public health and the acute care health system of hospitals, doctors, nurses, emergency services, pharmacies, nursing homes and other providers of care. The rapid spread of the virus throughout the country in 2020 placed a substantial strain on hospitals in particular, and the need to monitor health system capacity was immediate. The CDC launched a data module in its hospital surveillance system in order to collect data on critical hospital capacity indicators and used this data to help inform decisions of providers and public health officials at the local and state level to support efficient use of beds and ventilators. Hospitals were able to make decisions in real time about where to re-direct ambulances when needed, to expand bed and ICU capacity for COVID-19 patients, to restrict elective procedures, and to ration services when necessary due to lack of capacity.

COVID-19 highlighted one of the key reasons for the importance of strengthening the relationship and communication channels between public health agencies and the hospital system. The 2012 the IOM report *Primary Care and Public Health: Exploring Integration to Improve Population Health*, which was referenced earlier in this chapter, encouraged both sectors of healthcare (public and private) to collaborate in the interests of improving the population's health status through coordination, data sharing, and integration of services. COVID-19 became a stark reminder of the critical importance of this collaboration.

10.7 Summary

The role of public health is an important one in the context of healthcare delivery in the United States. Both the public and private sectors share goals and responsibilities for the health of communities and of individuals. While the public health orientation is primarily on population health and that of the healthcare delivery system is primarily focused on the individual, each is inherently tied to the other. Populations are made up of individuals, and individuals can have substantial impact on populations (e.g., in the spread of disease). While the early history of public health and healthcare delivery systems were integrally tied together, that relationship fragmented as the private sector of healthcare delivery grew and as the growing population demanded increasing attention to health hazards and overall health status. Following major disasters in the United States (e.g., hurricane Katrina, fires in California, floods in the Midwest, a bridge collapse in Minnesota) and with the threat of major acts of terrorism (e.g., 9/11), it has become clear that linkages between the two sectors are critical to the health and safety of the population and of individuals. This demand is driving increased collaboration, information sharing, and information technology infrastructure to support the sharing and caring that is needed in times of crises and in the interests of improved health status of the population. Healthy People 2030 is just one initiative that reflects a wider participation in initiatives to achieve these ends. COVID-19 became a stark reminder of its importance.

References

1. CDC Foundation. *What is public health.* Available at www.cdcfoundation.org/what-public-health.
2. Committee on Integrating Primary Care and Public Health; Board on Population Health and Public Health Practice, Institute of Medicine. 2012 (Mar. 28). *Primary care and public health: Exploring integration to improve population health.* Washington, DC: National Academies Press. doi: 10.17226/13381. Available at https://pubmed.ncbi.nlm.nih.gov/24851288/.
3. Institute of Medicine. 2003. *The future of the public's health in the 21st century.* Washington, DC: The National Academies Press. https://doi.org/10.17226/10548.
4. HHS: Office of the Surgeon General. *U.S. Public Health Service Commissioned Corps.* Available at www.hhs.gov/surgeongeneral/corps/index.html.
5. L. Shattuck. 1949. Report of the sanitary commission of Massachusetts 1850. *JAMA,* 140(6): 576. doi: 10.1001/jama.1949.02900410072033. Available at https://jamanetwork.com/journals/jama/article-abstract/304733.

6. Agency for Healthcare Research and Quality. *About AHRQ*. Available at www.ahrq.gov/cpi/about/mission/index.html.
7. Agency for Toxic Substances and Disease Registry. Available at www.astcr.cdc.gov.
8. Centers for Disease Control and Prevention. *Mission, role and pledge*. Available at www.cdc.gov/about/organization/mission.htm.
9. Food and Drug Administration. *What we do*. Available at www.fda.gov/about-fda/what-we-do.
10. Health Resources and Services Administration. *About HRSA*. Available at www.hrsa.gov/about/index.html.
11. Indian Health Service. *About IHS*. Available at www.ihs.gov/aboutihs/.
12. National Institutes of Health. *Mission and goals*. Available at www.nih.gov/about-nih/what-we-do/mission-goals.
13. Substance Abuse and Mental Health Services Administration. *About us*. Available at www.samhsa.gov/about-us.
14. Administration for Children and Families. *What we do*. Available at www.acf.hhs.gov/about.
15. Administration for Community Living. *Organizational history*. Available at https://acl.gov/about-acl/history.
16. Healthy People 2030. *Leading health indicators*. Available at https://health.gov/healthypeople/objectives-and-data/leading-health-indicators.
17. Merriam-Webster. *Pandemic*. Available at www.merriam-webster.com/dictionary/pandemic.

Chapter 11

Medical Science and Information Technology

11.1 Introduction

As in so many fields, technology is an accelerator of new development and innovation. Because of it, the field of medicine progressed over the last century from having a basic understanding of infection and its causes to the ability to conquer infection and to the continuing incredible advances that have occurred in medicine. We can perform multiple organ transplants successfully, reattach limbs after they have been severed, prolong life with procedures and drugs that were unheard of only decades ago. We have a plethora of other life-saving and enhancing medical interventions available and more coming to market continuously. Because of advances in science and technology, the average life span in the U.S. almost doubled in the last century from 46.3 years of age to 78.7, and the infant mortality rate dropped significantly in the U.S. and other developed countries.

The need to improve quality of care and to expand access to care and control the rate of cost increases in healthcare required that providers move into the digital data and information era. With the impetus of federal dollars in 2009 to incentivize the implementation of clinical information technology, aka, the electronic health record (EHR), hospitals and doctors acquired and implemented an EHR. Within a decade most U.S. hospitals had transitioned to an EHR, and a high proportion of doctors had done so as well. The increased volume and complexity of information that is generated at the bedside and in other clinical settings and the need to pass that information

DOI: 10.4324/9781003202950-11

from provider to provider, to improve the safety of patient care, respond to the many and varied payer programs that dominate U.S. healthcare financing, and improve the efficiency and effectiveness of care, made implementation of healthcare information technology (HIT) mandatory.

Both of these areas in medical care, i.e., advances in medical science and deployment of IT, consume huge investments and require time and process change. In this chapter, both of these technology areas will be briefly introduced. Each is a vast field and will require further study by the person whose professional life in healthcare management brings them into day-to-day involvement with Healthcare IT and/or advances in medical technology.

11.2 The Science of Medicine

The science of medicine is comprised of a wide array of procedures, tools, devices, and interventions that are used to diagnose and treat medical conditions. In this section, we will focus briefly on pharmaceuticals, research, genomics, and medical devices.

11.2.1 Pharmaceuticals

Pharmaceutical companies are primarily focused on the development and sale of drugs that prevent infections, cure diseases, and maintain health in individuals and the population. Over the past several decades, the pharmaceutical industry has advanced the field of bioscience and developed a plethora of new drugs that address life-threatening diseases. The industry has built the scientific foundations to craft even more pharmaceutical interventions that focus on what are still intractable diseases. For example, the vaccines for the coronavirus (COVID-19) were developed in an unusually short time span because of prior vaccine research that had been done. Because of the research investment in new drugs, innovation in the health sciences has resulted in dramatic changes in the ability to treat disease and improve the quality of life. Expenditures on pharmaceuticals have grown faster than other major components of the health care system since the late 1990s. Consequently, the debates on rising healthcare costs and the development of new medical technologies have focused increasingly on the pharmaceutical industry, which is both a major participant in the healthcare industry and a major source of advances in health care technologies. (1)

New drugs come to market on an ongoing basis as pharmaceutical companies and researchers discover and formulate new compounds to address specific health conditions. However, the process of getting those new drugs to market is complex, time consuming, and very costly. Currently it costs, on average, over $2.5 billion for a pharmaceutical manufacturer to get a drug from the laboratory to the pharmacy. The process for drug development and approval is long and risky, but with final approval, the manufacturer can market the patented drug product. After a patent is issued to a drug maker it is valid for 20 years after the drug's invention and no less than 17 years from when the patent is issued. During this time they have exclusive right to the drug's formulation and can price it in the U.S. without restrictions. But after that time, other drug makers are eligible to develop and market the same formula under a generic brand.

11.2.1.1 Clinical Trials Research

The clinical trials process from laboratory through clinical trials to FDA approval and into the retail or hospital pharmacy takes an average of 15 years for each drug. Less than 25 percent of drugs that begin a phase I clinical trial actually succeed in getting to market. Most of the drug development process occurs in the laboratory and in human clinical trials. The development process proceeds through pre-clinical research and clinical trials prior to applying to the FDA for approval. That approval is completed by the FDA's Center for Drug Evaluation and Research (CDER). In 2020, CDER approved 53 novel drugs, which are "innovative products that serve previously unmet medical needs or otherwise significantly help to advance patient care and public health." (2) The major steps in the FDA approval process are:

11.2.1.1.1 Step 1: Preclinical Research

The first step of a clinical trial is the preclinical research. This phase begins in the laboratory with teams of scientists working together to create and preliminarily test compounds that will treat a physiological condition. This research includes animal studies that evaluate how the compound works in a living organism. This phase may be completed in short-term testing of two weeks to three months or long-term testing of a few weeks to several years depending on the planned use of the substance. Once the preclinical research is complete, the drug sponsor can complete an Investigational New Drug application (IND) and submit this to the CDER. (2) The IND approval allows the manufacturer to proceed with human clinical trials. INDs are also used to request approval in "emergency use" situations in order for the CDER to authorize use of an experimental drug when time is of the essence. (3) Following preclinical research and IND approval, new drug research moves into a four-phase clinical trials process.

11.2.1.1.2 Phase I: Clinical Studies

Phase I of clinical studies involves the initial introduction of an investigational new drug into humans. These studies are typically conducted in 20 to 80 healthy volunteer subjects and are designed to determine the drug's effect on humans, including the metabolic and pharmacological actions, the side effects associated with increasing doses, and, if possible, to gain early evidence on effectiveness, and any potential early indications of toxicity of the drug. Phase I trials typically take from one to one and a half years to complete. If they do not reveal unacceptable levels of toxicity, then the drug generally moves into phase II of the clinical trials.

11.2.1.1.3 Phase II: Clinical Studies

Phase II includes the early controlled clinical studies in several hundred test subjects (people with the disease or condition that the drug targets). In these studies, the researchers seek to obtain preliminary data on the effectiveness of the drug for a particular indication or indications in patients. This phase of testing also helps determine the common short-term side effects and risks associated with the drug. Typically, phase II of the clinical trials takes about two years to complete. About one-third of drugs introduced into phase II complete this phase successfully.

11.2.1.1.4 Phase III: Clinical Studies

In phase III, research is expanded with controlled and uncontrolled trials. The objective of this phase is to study the effectiveness, safety, and overall benefit-risk relationship of the drug. Phase III studies include several hundreds to thousands of subjects and are performed to provide an adequate basis for extrapolating the results to the general population and transmitting that information to the physician through labeling. Phase III takes about three years to complete. The success rate for drugs in phase III is 70 percent to 90 percent.

11.2.1.1.5 Phase IV: Clinical Studies

Every new drug completes a new drug application (NDA) process and must be approved by the FDA prior to being marketed by its sponsor company. An NDA includes all preclinical animal testing and human clinical trial data and analyses. Following approval, phase IV trials continue for years. During this time, the drug can be used commercially, but the sponsor is required to perform long-term data collection. Thousands of patients use the drug over several years, and data from those patients and their doctors are used to learn about the treatment's long-term side effects, risks, benefits, and optimal use, or to test the product in different populations of people such as children or the elderly.

11.2.1.2 Challenges for the Pharmaceutical Sector

Despite the numerous amazing drugs that have been developed over the past decades, pharmaceutical companies also face criticism and challenges throughout their markets, particularly in pricing. Increases in drug prices, and in some cases drastic increases, can cause life-saving drugs to be out of reach of patients who rely on them. There have been examples of egregious price gauging in pharmaceuticals that have tainted the industry in the minds of consumers and have caused innovative drugs to be inaccessible to patients who need them. Insurers often deny coverage of extremely costly medications and, for most patients for whom out-of-pocket payment is their only financial recourse, the drugs are out of reach. In part, this is due to the patent protection that is given for drugs. With that patent protection, the company holding the patent for a specific drug can price that drug as they wish. It's reasonable to expect price increases in drugs as in products in other market sectors, however, the U.S. does not have a consistent approach to ensuring access to life-saving drugs for those who cannot afford them.

In a corollary price issue, overseas markets often face drug prices that make certain drugs inaccessible. On the other hand, some countries purchase drugs from pharmaceutical companies at prices established by the government. In the U.S. drug prices are significantly higher while Medicare, the leading payer for drugs in the country, is still prohibited from negotiating drug prices for its enrollees.

The pharmaceutical sector also faces challenges related to increasing specialization in medicine. Markets for highly specialized drugs are narrow as the number of patients is relatively small. This means the drug company does not have the profit opportunity of, for example, blockbuster drugs that target a high-volume population market.

The opioid crisis has particularly taken a toll on the pharmaceutical industry. While not all pharmaceutical companies have been found to be at fault in the opioid crisis, the fallout from one company's role has been felt in others.

11.2.2 Biomedical Research

Biomedical research is core to the development of pharmaceutical products, but it's role also encompasses the work of scientists who "use biotechnology methods to study diseases and biological processes" to "better understand the causes and cure of illnesses" through the drugs, vaccines and procedures that are available to medical providers. (4) Biomedical research is key to developing an understanding of complex living organisms and how they function down to the cellular level.

Funding for biomedical research comes from both public and private resources. The National Institutes of Health (NIH), the largest public funding source for biomedical research, invests over $32 billion in it annually. In the private sector, pharmaceutical, biotechnology, and medical device companies fund research and development, with some support from federal sources such as happened in the development of the COVID-19 vaccines. Some lesser amounts of research are also carried out or funded by private nonprofit foundations.

The National Institutes of Health (NIH) is part of the U.S. Department of Health and Human Services and is the primary agency of the government for biomedical research. Its goal is to expand knowledge in medical and associated sciences to help prevent, detect, diagnose, and cure disease and disability. NIH is made up of 27 Institutes and Centers, each of which has a specific focus. Overall, NIH is divided into intramural divisions and an extramural division. Internally, the NIH has almost 6,000 researchers who conduct research at the NIH main campus in Bethesda, Maryland. The Office of Extramural Research (OER) is in charge of the funding of biomedical research outside of NIH. The NIH funds almost 50,000 competitive grants for more than 300,000 researchers at over 2,500 medical schools, universities, and other research organizations. (5)

11.2.3 Genomics

The National Human Genome Research Institute defines genetics as "the study of all of a person's genes (the genome), including interactions of those genes with each other and with the person's environment." (6) A human genome is an organism's complete set of DNA. It includes all the genetic material (DNA) of an organism.

Through the Human Genome Project, we learned that human beings have about 20,500 genes coiled in DNA and housed in each individual's trillions of cells. Although all the human genome sequences were completed in April 2003, much continues to be learned about the essential component of the cell "protein" and the complex network it creates. For major diseases such as cancer, heart disease, arthritis, and diabetes, the cellular and molecular changes involved in the development of these conditions are so complicated that better understanding of the basic molecular and cellular mechanisms is necessary in their diagnosis, treatment, and prevention. Through biomedical research, the mechanisms of disease can be thoroughly examined and understood, and diseases will be more likely to be diagnosed and cured at an early stage. Early intervention can result in avoidance of expensive medical diagnostics and surgical procedures, improvement in the quality of life for patients and reducing healthcare costs. (7)

Having access to the human genome sequence is a powerful tool in understanding the pathogenesis of disease. The ability to identify candidate genes, hypothesize about their function, and identify the same or similar genes in other organisms that permit experimentation has greatly accelerated the pace of research. As dramatic as these advances have been, however, far more remains to be learned about how genes affect human health. The field of pharmacogenomics is poised for this future.

Pharmacogenomics is the study of how an individual's genetic inheritance affects the body's response to drugs. This field holds the promise of *precision medicine*, in which research and development of medical treatment is tailored to small stratified groups of individuals. Environment, diet, age, lifestyle, and state of health can all influence a person's response to medicines, but understanding an individual's genetic makeup is thought to be the key to creating personalized drugs with greater efficacy and safety. It has the potential to transform the quality, safety, and value of healthcare.

Cancers, in particular, have been the focus of early development and adoption of precision medicine. From an ongoing perspective, researchers in the field are focused on diseases with both genetic and environmental causes including autism, heart disease, diabetes, and obesity, in addition to cancer. (7)

Precision medicine is possible due largely to extensive data availability through the use of information technology and technological advances. The technological advances that enable precision medicine include the electronic medical record (EMR), mobile medical devices and monitors, storage technology improvements, and high-performance computing technologies.

In order for precision medicine to become more available and accessible to the population, it needs to be integrated into medical school curriculum and into widespread clinical practice, reimbursement structures must be developed and implemented to support it, and public policies and legislation must foster it. With widespread adoption, precision medicine has the potential to improve the return on dollars invested in healthcare.

The healthcare and pharmaceutical industries have never before been faced with greater pressure–both internal and external–to speed drug production and move toward precision medicine. Meanwhile, new discoveries in genomics and the widespread use of high-throughput research technologies are producing massive amounts of data to enable better understanding of disease. These forces all contribute to researchers' and medical providers' increasing need to leverage information assets and align their clinical and research environments.

From an ethical perspective, precision medicine raises concerns relative to confidentiality and potential discrimination against individuals by insurers and employers. From a broader societal perspective, ethical questions also arise regarding privacy, informed consent, disclosure, social justice, and other issues. (8) The Genetic Information Nondiscrimination Act, also known as GINA, of 2008, is designed to protect Americans against discrimination in health insurance and employment and to pave the way for people to take full advantage of the promise of precision medicine without fear of discrimination.

11.3 Information Technology

11.3.1 Introduction

Earlier, we discussed only a few key advances in medical science. Those advances can only happen with the incredible amount of data that is generated electronically to drive their development. In other words, information is central to medical science and medical care delivery. Accurate and complete information are essential to realizing the opportunities that are in medicine's future, the improved quality and comprehensiveness of care and reductions in the rate of increase in the cost of care.

During the many decades of computerization in other sectors of the economy, healthcare provider organizations seriously lagged behind electronic recording of clinical data. The investment to achieve ubiquitous adoption and use of electronic health records was enormous both in treasure and in human involvement. The federal government made the funding commitment to health IT in the HITECH Act of 2009. This legislation mandated the implementation of health data standards to be used by hospitals, physicians, and other providers of healthcare and for required reporting to be done electronically. It forced a move away from paper records. HITECH provided financial incentives to providers to acquire and adopt electronic health records. In the following decade, the rate of adoption of EHRs dramatically accelerated in the U.S. among hospitals and doctors.

EHRs support the recording and sharing of clinical and other patient data among physicians and health systems. However, the sharing of data is reliant upon interoperable systems that can "talk" to one another, and upon the readiness of physicians, hospitals, and other providers to share data. The lack of interoperability continues to be a barrier to full sharing of information from hospital system to hospital system throughout the country. When a patient moves geographically or goes to a different provider than the one at which they have a medical record established, that record is typically not accessible by the new provider because the two hospital systems do not have interoperable EHRs.

In most cases, the patient must repeat the same information for input into the records of the new provider or the patient and doctor wait while the fax machine, or even the postal service, delivers the information in hard copy to the new provider's office. In that scenario, not only must the patient wonder about the adequacy of the information that is accessed by hard copy but must also be concerned that the provider is hamstrung by the lack of timely and complete information that would make them more efficient and productive. In the absence of needed medical test and diagnostic results, the patient is subject to duplicate testing, prescription errors, burdensome administrative requirements, inefficiencies, and other costly consequences. As healthcare costs consume over 17 percent of the U.S. GDP and continue to rise and while the quality of clinical outcomes in the U.S. still lags behind other developed countries (see Chapter 2), the imperative for the fully functional and interoperable shared electronic health record (EHR) grows.

The American Hospital Association (AHA) summed up the problem:

> Research has shown that certain kinds of technology (IT)–such as computerized physician order entry (CPOE), computerized decision support systems, and bar coding for medication administration–can limit errors and improve care by ensuring that the right information is available in the right place at the right time to treat patients.

(9)

11.3.2 The EHR and Healthcare Quality Improvement

The need for systemic transformation of healthcare delivery in the U.S. became evident with rising healthcare costs that were typically outstripping the consumer price index year after year. Additionally, the IOM Report *To Err is Human* and its findings regarding deaths in hospitals due to unintended causes and subsequent reports on this topic focused on strategies to address both the cost and quality problems that were affecting the economy, productivity, and health status in the country. The drumbeat for the fully interoperable EHR continues from all sectors of society–employers, consumers, government, researchers, payers, and even healthcare organizations.

- *Employers* want to assure that the money they are spending on employee health insurance supports the productivity of a healthy workforce. Rising healthcare costs compel employers to transfer more of the cost of insurance onto their employees. They need elimination of duplication in medical testing, reduction in errors, and greater efficiency in healthcare. The electronic sharing of data is key to eliminating the paper record and the administrative burden that it incurs and to improving outcomes by reducing errors and duplication of services.

- *Consumers* want information. As they reach deeper into their own pockets to pay for health insurance and out-of-pocket expenses, they need information that will help them make better choices. They also want to see more coordination of their care by their doctors, hospitals, and other providers.

- *Government* requires the implementation of EHRs in provider organizations across the country and in 2009 legislated the collection and electronic reporting of clinical data and funded the implementation and use of EHRs. Policy makers are also pressed to reduce the burden of health care costs on the economy while also making healthcare services equitably available to all sectors of society.

- *Payers* were, for a long time, among the prime movers for the EHR. The EHR supports the transfer of data, thereby reducing the administrative workforce needed to handle paper; it supports the accuracy of data and billing statements; it supports the reduction in duplication of testing that drives up healthcare costs; and through data reporting and analysis, supports quality improvement.

■ Finally, *healthcare providers* recognized that they needed to move from paper records to electronic records in order to improve quality of care, efficiency cost control and patient satisfaction. Systems that support CPOE and medication management offer the opportunity to establish new processes to improve the accuracy of ordering, filling, and administering drugs, IVs, and IV additives and, ultimately, of reduction in errors. Electronic systems also are essential to supporting the accurate transfer of medical record information when patients are transitioned from one care provider to another (e.g., from emergency room, to surgery, to ICU) and to achieve strategic organizational and financial management goals.

Overall, the implementation and use of the EMR has proven to be central to improving the safety, efficiency, and effectiveness of medical care. Chapter 9 discussed the scope and impact of medical errors and the number of deaths that occur in hospitals due to preventable medical errors. These errors arise from things such as hand-written orders for drugs that cannot be deciphered; from errors that occur in the transition of patient care from one provider to the next. They are also the result of errors in patient identification in treatment or medication administration; of miscommunicated clinical information; and of errors at other process points. The electronic health record is important to improve patient safety.

11.3.3 Components of the EHR

The EHR is comprised of a complex system of hardware, functions, and software applications. Its basic components include:

■ The *patient management component* that provides functionality for patient registration, admission, and discharge. After an initial registration with a provider, the patient record is assigned a medical record number in the Master Patient Index. This is an ID that is unique to that patient and will follow the patient in future encounters with the same provider. The patient record will integrate all the clinical information linked to the patient by use of the unique ID.
■ The *clinical component* that is comprised of sub-components including nursing, CPOE, pharmacy, and electronic documentation. The latter is used for operative and consultation notes and for other notes such as the patient's history and physical.

- The *Laboratory Information System (LIS)* that records test results directly from the pathology laboratory analytical machines and integrates with billing and with tests ordered by doctors and other clinicians.
- The *Radiology Information System (RIS)* that is used for receiving orders from clinicians and for recording images and results. A major part of the RIS is Picturing Archiving and Communications System (PACS) for the recording of images and making those available to doctors and other clinicians.
- The *billing system* that captures from the various system components all charges that are generated during the patient care encounter and submits them to payers.
- The *scheduling system* that supports all scheduling of patient visits, staffing, surgical suites, and other testing services in the provider organization.

11.3.4 Health Information Exchange

Health information exchange (HIE) refers to the interoperable technology and process infrastructure that supports sharing clinical and other patient data within a geographic region and among the organizationally unrelated providers of care in that region. Information exchange is key to improving quality, reducing costs, and achieving more efficiency and effectiveness in healthcare delivery. HIE enables providers to

- "Access and confidentially share patients' vital medical history, no matter where patients are receiving care–specialists' offices, labs, or emergency rooms.
- Provide safer, more effective care tailored to patients' unique medical needs."

(10)

As individual healthcare provider organizations have developed and implemented the EHR, HIE initiatives have been under way in geographic regions across the country to develop the technical and governance infrastructure to support sharing of data throughout the region. In many states, these HIEs are funded with both state and federal dollars. The ultimate objective of HIEs is to create the capability and environment through which an interoperable Nationwide Health Information Network (NwHIN) can be developed to support the sharing of health information among providers and patients

nationwide. This widespread sharing of information provides the opportunity for better medical decision-making at the point of care and allows
providers and patients to avoid readmissions, decrease duplication of testing,
avoid medication errors, and improve diagnosis. In other words, it supports
significant improvements in the quality of patient care.

Currently clinical data exchange through HIEs happens between providers who are in the same organization and is particularly useful to those large
provider organizations that are geographically dispersed. Most of the shared
data is related to radiology images and lab results. Expansion in sharing of
clinical notes and patient summaries is not ubiquitous but is progressing.

11.3.5 The Personal Health Record

The personal health record (PHR) is a collection of information about an
individual's health and an opportunity for patient engagement in the care
process. The PHR is a component of the EHR in which the patient has control, i.e., it is that person's individual record and as such data can be entered
into it by the patient, and it can be accessed by the patient at any point.
Sharing of that information is under the control of the patient who can give
providers access as they choose to do so. PHRs enhance the ability of a
patient to see a new provider because, rather than having to carry paper
records or have them faxed to the new provider, the patient can simply give
that provider access to the record, albeit with limited information.

A number of employers have made the PHR available to their employees
as a part of their health plan in order to encourage the employee to take
charge of their healthcare and to assure consistent and complete information not only about their medical care but also about their wellness activities
(exercise, alternative healthcare, and so on).

A key ingredient of the PHR is its ability to integrate or interface with
the EHR, and its impact on medical discussion and decisions at the point of
care. It supports the patient's full engagement in decision-making by including the needs, values, and input of the patient.

The PHR is tethered to the EHR of the provider organization from which
the patient gets care. If they go to different providers that are not organizationally related, they may have multiple PHRs that are not integrated with
interoperable software. When a patient goes to a provider outside the network that provider has the ability to access the patient's PHR at the "home
provider" with the patient's permission and access code.

11.3.6 Types of Information Systems in Healthcare

The healthcare IT environment consists of three major system components: application software, hardware, and network connectivity. It also requires information systems in two major domains: the administrative or business functions of healthcare and the clinical functions. Healthcare software must support the many varied functions in each of these two domains, and it must serve to integrate information between both domains. In order to have a fully functioning EHR, the systems need to support full sharing of information, on a need-to-know basis, among clinicians, administrators, patients, and others who are involved in care regardless of their geographic location or the venue of care (hospital, physician's office, rehabilitation, ambulatory center, etc.)

This presents a particularly complex problem for IT developers in healthcare. It requires systems to support point-of-care decision-making, which occurs when the clinician is seeing the patient, diagnosing and ordering tests, providing medication, or performing other clinical functions. At the point of care, data needs to come together from a complex array of clinical systems that support a broad array of diagnostic data, patient history and clinical notes. This requires data warehouses that not only store complex data but also have the capacity to support evidence-based medicine by making clinical research and findings available at the clinician's fingertips on the case at hand, so that he or she has immediate access to the latest research findings and to best practices.

The major categories of healthcare IT systems are clinical systems and administrative systems. Clinical systems serve in the patient care settings such as at the bedside, in the surgical suite, the emergency department, the laboratory, radiology, pharmacy the doctor's office, and so on. Administrative systems, on the other hand, support the business and management functions of the organization–areas such as billing, accounts payable, reporting, human resources, supplies management, and so on. Not only are these two domains the major focus of integrated information systems, but other functions in healthcare also need to be supported. This includes activities such as research and education, which are highly reliant on the data that information systems can make available. The design, development, and implementation of fully integrated information systems for healthcare providers are as complex as the organizations themselves.

11.3.7 *Health IT Standards*

There are major challenges on the path to achieving the fully interoperable EHR, and standards are essential to achieve that interoperability. Standards are defined as "agreed-upon methods for connecting systems together. Standards may pertain to security, data transport, data format or structure, or the meanings of codes or terms. Standards are defined, updated, and maintained by standards development organizations (SDOs) through a collaborative process involving the audience that will be using the standards." (11)

Key to standards development is achieving consensus among the many SDOs, and their constituents. The healthcare industry has at least 40 SDOs that are designated to develop specifications and standards to support healthcare informatics, information exchange, systems integration, and a wide spectrum of healthcare applications. Some of the major SDOs are listed in Table 11.1. Most SDOs are accredited by the American National Standards Institute (ANSI) whose accreditation process requires that standards be developed and promulgated with openness, consensus, balance, and due process. (12) The SDO must also comply with ANSI oversight. Standards apply primarily in four areas of healthcare IT. As described in Table 11.1, they include content standards, structure standards, messaging standards, and functional standards.

Standards development in healthcare faces a number of challenges including:

1. Security and privacy: Security of information is critical both to the organization and to the patient. Under HIPAA, healthcare organizations that are engaged in the electronic transfer of data (e.g., billing to payers for services provided to patients) are required to have systems in place to guard the privacy of patient data. They are subject to substantial penalties for each instance in which patient data are accessed by anyone other than a person who has a "need to know." Yet, as is evident from violations that are reported both in healthcare and in other sectors of the economy, securing data with absolute assurance that security will not be violated is challenging. In healthcare, there is a wide diversity of human beings, both inside the provider organization and outside, who, with their own ID and password, can access patient data. The

Table 11.1   Major Healthcare IT Standards Organizations

Global Standards Organizations		
Acronym	*Organization*	*Standard*
ISO	International Organization for Standardization	Healthcare and others
IEC	International Electrotechnical Commission	Computer
ITU	International Telecommunication Union	Telecommunications
HL7	Health Level 7	EHR, messaging, and communication
UN EDIFACT	UN Electronic Data Interchange for Finance, Administration, Commerce and Transportation	EDI
DICOM	Digital Imaging and Communication in Medicine	Medical imaging
IEEE	Institute of Electrical and Electronic Engineers	Network and device communication
CEN	Committee for European Normalisation (European Committee for Standardization)	ISO
OMG	Object Management Group	UML, CORBA
WHO	World Health Organization	Classification of diseases
IHTSDO	International Health Terminology Standards Development Organization	SNOMED-CT
LOINC	Logical Observation Identifiers Names and Codes	Laboratory
IHE	Integrating the Healthcare Enterprise	Interoperable profiles

organization is reliant on technology security, education, trust, and policies that carry heavy penalties for employees or other stakeholders who violate that trust.

2. Data sharing: While the healthcare industry, providers and vendors, work through the challenges of designing and developing data sharing networks, the human element in the sharing of data is yet another challenge to the implementation of the interoperable EHR. There is reluctance among providers, hospitals, and physicians alike to share

with other providers what they view as proprietary data. They are concerned about how the data will be used, how that data might be analyzed to make provider comparisons for quality and efficacy, and for the security of the data from hacking, leaks, and other potential vulnerabilities.

As healthcare moves forward from the pandemic events of 2020, the focus on information sharing has intensified. At the federal level, the interest in managing cohorts of patients will more intensely drive the need for improved and expanded reporting to the federal government in order to gain a better understanding of promoting the health of populations as compared to that of individuals. Providers need to capture and aggregate information and provide it to the federal government to enable faster response to population health issues.

11.3.8 Digital Health

The coronavirus pandemic turned 2020 into a year of dramatic change in healthcare delivery. Health IT infrastructure (IT hardware and software and communications technologies) played a key role in that change. Telemedicine became almost a commonplace method of clinician-patient consultation overnight. While neither party had previously been comfortable with telemedicine as a method of conducting office visits, they quickly learned and accepted it due to COVID-19 practice restrictions and needs for personal safety. Clinicians turned to the mobile digital platforms already available to them, and while virtual visits continue to "settle" into common practice, the technology is being honed to intuitively accommodate those visits, expand access to care, and enhance the clinician-patient relationship. Payers have already expanded payment structures of virtual visits, and that process is likely to continue.

Following the 2020 healthcare experience with COVID-19, supply chain structures have taken on new importance to hospitals and other care providers. The lack of personal protective equipment and ventilators was particularly glaring and alarming in the first year of the pandemic. Some executives look to predictive analytics to not only support long- and short-term strategy development, but also to assess future states of market demand in order to ensure adequacy in supply chain flexibility and preparedness for future population mass health events such as widespread climate disasters and potential epidemics or pandemics.

Additionally, the need for timely public health reporting became evident during 2020, as well as other government-required reporting. As a society, initiatives to ensure early data capture and reporting in order to assess and respond to health issues that are on the horizon came to be recognized as vitally important. In the future some of that data will come from consumer wearables and other device sensors that can provide real-time data on the individual's health. The demand for these will grow along with peoples' need and willingness to be informed of and share their personal health data. The pace of data collection and the development of storing and analysis capability will require new applications and capacity.

Other new technologies that are being driven by a vision of what can be possible and put in practice in the future are also evolving. New technologies are already gaining traction and others are on the horizon and/or being developed to new and more complex applications. For example:

■ Nanotechnology uses nanoparticles to reach cells inside the body where they can diagnose diseases or deliver medicines with precision. For instance, nanotechnology can be used to correct abnormal growth of tissues or cells in the human body. Nanobots are, effectively, microscopic robots designed to carry out specific functions such as the delivery of medications to the exact cells that the medication targets. To offer a sense of scale of nanobots: there are 25,400,000 nanometers in an inch.

■ Robotics: Robots are increasingly common in manufacturing. In healthcare, they are known mostly for their applications in surgical suites and the movement of clinical and nursing supplies in hospitals. The future of healthcare will be more populated by robots in such activities as dispensing medication, disinfecting patient rooms, providing assistance in surgery, and keeping long term patients actively engaged. In these and other way, robots will enable doctors, nurses, and other clinicians to apply their skills in direct care of patients rather than spending time in more mundane and simple tasks.

■ Artificial Intelligence (AI) is used to analyze large amounts of data and provide insight in the diagnosis and prevention of disease. AI can access and integrate data from the EHR to recognize patterns and support better decision-making. AI will have ever increasing applications in healthcare.

These are only a few of the ways in technology is poised to transform the healthcare system and healthcare delivery at the bedside and in the clinic. It has the potential to support fundamental change in healthcare taking medical delivery from the model of responding to illness to one of maintaining well-being. This has profound implications for the entire healthcare sector of the economy, for employers, and for the individual.

11.4 Summary

The future of healthcare is tied to its ongoing scientific research and to the IT infrastructure that is key to its future, efficiency, effectiveness, and quality initiatives to protect the safety of patients while in hospitals and other venues of medical care. The potential for genomics to dramatically change the way in which medical care is delivered is awesome–the development of personalized healthcare can revolutionize medical care in the capability it has to address health problems by delivering solutions that are designed for the individual's genetic structure. However, the ability to take advantage of this research and to get it to the clinical setting is dependent upon the full implementation and interoperability of the EHR. While the United States is making incredible investments in genomics and healthcare IT, the future can only be shaped by the will to make the results available to all and by the readiness to accept a new way of looking at medicine and at each person's responsibility and potential to control and manage his or her own health.

References

1. J.A. DiMasi, R. Hansen and H.G. Grabowski. 2003. The price of innovation: New estimated of drug development costs. *Journal of Health Economics*, 22: 151–185.
2. Food and Drug Administration (FDA). Available at www.drugs.com/fda-approval-process.html.
3. E.R. Colgate. 2019 (Oct. 23). FDA investigational new drug applications for sponsor-investigators. *University of Vermont, Larner College of Medicine, Research Professionals Network*. Available at www.bumc.bu.edu/crro/files/2019/10/RPN_-IND_Presentation_Colgate_2019.10.23-V2.pdf.
4. A. Scott. 2020 (Dec. 26). *What is biomedical research?* Available at www.nhinbre.org/what-is-biomedical-research/.

5. National Institutes of Health. *What we do*. Available at www.nih.gov/about-nih/what-we-do/budget.

6. National Human Genome Research Institute. A brief guide to genomics. Available at: https://www.genome.gov/about-genomics/fact-sheets/A-Brief-Guide-to-Genomics.

7. CDC. *Pharmacogenomics: What does it mean for your health?* Available at www.cdc.gov/genomics/disease/pharma.htm.

8. J.N. Batten. 2018 (Sept.). How stratification unites ethical issues in precision health. *AMA Journal of Ethics*, 20(9): E798–803. Available at www.fda.gov/media/95661/download#:~:text=Novel%20drugs%20are%20often%20innovative%20products%20that%20serve,have%20never%20been%20approved%20before.%20However%2C%20in%20some.

9. American Hospital Association (AHA). 2005. *Forward momentum: Hospital use of information technology*. Available at www.cssolutionsinc.com/downloads/Whitepapers/FINALNonEmbITSurvey105.pdf.

10. HealthIT.Gov. *Health information exchange*. Available at www.healthit.gov/topic/health-it-and-health-information-exchange-basics/health-information-exchange.

11. Office of the National Coordinator. *HealthIT.gov: Health IT standards*. Available at www.healthit.gov/topic/standards-technology/health-it-standards#:~:text=Health%20IT%20Standards%20Like%20other%20industries%2C%20health%20care,structure%2C%20or%20the%20meanings%20of%20codes%20or%20terms.

12. American National Standards Institute. *Introduction*. Available at https://ansi.org/about/roles.

Index

Note: Page numbers in *italics* indicate a figure and page numbers in **bold** indicate a table on the corresponding page.

Printed in Great Britain
by Amazon

23690722R00123